BETTY KRAWCZYK

LOCK Me Up
or Let Me GO

The Protests,
Arrest and
Trial of an
Environmental
Activist

 PRESS GANG
AN IMPRINT OF RAINCOAST BOOKS

Press Gang Books and Raincoast Books gratefully acknowledge the financial
support of the Government of Canada through the Book Publishing
Industry Development Program and the Canada Council for the Arts. We
also acknowledge the assistance of the Government of British Columbia
through the British Columbia Arts Council.

Edited by Barbara Kuhne
Text design by Val Speidel

National Library of Canada Cataloguing in Publication Data

Krawczyk, Betty Shiver, 1928–
   Lock me up or let me go

   ISBN 1-55192-465-x

   1. Krawczyk, Betty Shiver, 1928- 2. Environmentalists—
British Columbia—Biography. 3. Women political activists—British
Columbia—Biography. I. Title.
GE56.K72A3 2002   363.7'0092   C2001-911676-4

Libraray of Congress Catalogue Number: 2002102383

Press Gang
An Imprint of Raincoast Books
9050 Shaughnessy Street
Vancouver, British Columbia
Canada   V6P 6E5
www.raincoast.com

In the United States:
Publishers Group West
1700 Fourth Street
Berkeley, California 94710

At Raincoast Books we are committed to protecting the environment and to
the responsible use of natural resources. We are acting on this commitment
by working with suppliers and printers to phase out our use of paper
produced from ancient forest. This book is one step towards that goal. It is
printed on 100% ancient-forest-free paper (100% post-consumer recycled),
processed chlorine- and acid-free, and supplied by New Leaf Paper. It is
printed with vegetable-based inks. For further information, visit our website
at www.raincoast.com. We are working with Markets Initiative (www.old-
growthfree.com) on this project.

1 2 3 4 5 6 7 8 9 10

Printed and bound in Canada by Houghton Boston

I dedicate this book to my daughter Marian Theresa
Krawczyk, who stood by me with unending patience
and humour—qualities she claims she was forced to
develop because she has such a weird mother.

I also dedicate this book to Barney Kern and
the Friends of the Elaho.

Contents

Chapter One / 7

Chapter Two / 25

Chapter Three / 43

Chapter Four / 57

Chapter Five / 69

Chapter Six / 77

Chapter Seven / 93

Chapter Eight / 103

Chapter Nine / 117

Chapter Ten / 137

Chapter Eleven / 153

Chapter Twelve / 169

Chapter Thirteen / 195

Afterword / 213

Acknowledgements / 217

Chapter One

May 19, 2000. Suzanne has just been escorted out of the courtroom by three sheriff's deputies—to thunderous applause from our supporters. She told the judge she didn't want to be tried by him, she wanted to be tried by the Squamish people. The Elaho Valley, where Suzanne and I were arrested, is traditional Squamish territory. The First Nations people are presently in negotiations with the government over land claims, and we both knew that Mr. Justice Parrett wasn't likely to agree that Suzanne could be tried by the Squamish elders. She was primarily making a protest, which is about all one can do in the legal pit we've been tossed into.

But at least the judge didn't attempt to make Suzanne stay in the courtroom against her will. He has already been through that with me. If a prisoner is determined to leave the courtroom when she is representing herself, the only two choices a judge has are to let her go or have her bound and gagged. Mr. Justice Parrett is not into the latter. I've tested him on that. Still, I find this judge's noticeable lack of empathy with young people's idealism bloody annoying. Mr. Justice Parrett seems to understand nothing of the depth of feeling many young people have for the remaining forests of British Columbia. I rise to my feet.

"Sir, I have a complaint," I say loudly. He is busy with his notebook. Judges are always writing in their notebooks.

"And what is your complaint, Mrs. Krawczyk?" Mr. Justice Parrett asks without looking up.

What is my complaint? This courtroom is my complaint, I want to yell, you are my complaint, the entire justice system of British Columbia is my complaint! We are hauled into this courtroom before you, sir, all eight of us, but we are forbidden to speak of why we are here, we can't talk about the Elaho Valley, about the thousand-year-old Douglas fir trees that are being clearcut as we speak by International Forest Products, commonly known as Interfor. The ancient Standing Ones are being torn from the earth and hauled away by massive death-dealing machines that scrape and mutilate the very bosom of the forest floor, obliterating the nests and burrows and hiding places and breeding grounds of fish and birds and beasts, many of which have not even been classified yet.

"Yes, Mrs. Krawczyk?" the judge asks. He has put down his pen and is looking at me. He is waiting. One mustn't keep the judge waiting. I have to make a decision here. Most of my co-accused have lawyers sitting at the counsel tables up front. Mr. Flanz, the Crown counsel, and the defence attorneys are ever so sneakily swivelling in their chairs to get a better view of the prisoner's box. They wear curious but apprehensive expressions. They are apparently wondering if anything else remarkable is about to occur in the prisoner's box after Suzanne's exit.

How regal the attorneys all look in their black robes with their important papers spread out before them on the long counsel tables, their heavy briefcases full of law tomes at the ready. I like these men. They're trying to do the right thing for their clients—if only the judge would give some indication of what that might be. I personally don't think there is going to be any right thing, which is why I have chosen to court the media and the public instead of only addressing the court. Impossible to romance a stone anyway, which is what Mr. Justice Parrett is. Somehow we must leap over this courtroom, this judge, and sail into the arms of the public.

I remember a recent poll that announced that 72 percent of the public favoured stronger government controls over industrial logging in B.C. forests. So at this point I could denounce the court, which for all practical purposes is Mr. Justice Parrett, and attempt to leave. But the attempted leaving would be a sham. There is no place to go except back up to the court cells, where I would be held until Suzanne and I are both driven back to Burnaby Correctional Centre for Women (BCCW). And of course I would be re-apprehended by the courtroom sheriffs, and I would be banished from the courtroom, which is much like expelling a student from school for playing hooky. I decide another courtroom banishment could hurt more than help at this juncture in the trial.

"I want to complain about the leg irons that Miss Jackson and I are locked into when we are brought to court from BCCW!" I blurt out.

The judge folds his arms on his massive desk with an air of resignation, of one who is much put upon.

"Mrs. Krawczyk, I will not interfere with the sheriff's department in their handling of prisoners," he says firmly, favouring me with a brief, tight, sour smile. That smile promises that I will pay for my part in the morning's drama. He thinks I have put Suzanne up to leaving the courtroom, that I am a bad influence on the young. He doesn't know Suzanne Jackson. She knows more about the flora and fauna of the Elaho Valley than I do. She's lived in the Elaho for months on end gathering data, witnessing the clearcutting of paradise, mourning the loss as she coped with the wet and the cold and the ever-present intimidation from loggers. Not to mention the bugs. Suzanne lived her beliefs long before I met her.

I take a deep breath. "And they take away my shoelaces," I go on as though I hadn't heard the judge. "This is not a good idea, sir, I tell you, it isn't a good idea."

I pause to take another deep breath, but not long enough for the judge to cut me off.

"The sheriffs take my shoelaces, sir, and then they handcuff me and put legs irons on me and then expect me, a seventy-one-year-old great-grandmother, to crawl on my hands and knees, if need be, into that police truck, and I'm telling you, sir, that is not a good idea ..."

I feel just a tad guilty about this. The sheriff's deputies who haul me around are actually more than middling careful about helping me into and out of the police wagon. And it isn't that I'm frail or so elderly. It's that my legs are short. I have the same trouble getting in and out of small, high-sided boats: I usually wind up having to jump from the bow rather than hoist over, as most longer-legged people do. And too often, I wind up in the water.

Which I fear is happening in this courtroom. The judge is giving me the evil eye.

"Mrs. Krawczyk," he begins with that exaggerated tone of patience and condescension that I have come to know so well. I can read his mental and emotional state as much from his body language as from what he is saying, but the mental and emotional forces behind these states are as mysterious as a Cajun gumbo. I take another deep breath.

"Okay, sir ... if the officers insist on using leg irons, I'll go along with that, but sir ... I want my shoelaces!"

There. That fixes him. For a brief moment he is totally perplexed. But he recovers quickly.

"Mrs. Krawczyk, is that all you have to say?"

"No, sir. This entire proceeding is unfair. Here I am, brought back before you, the same judge who issued the injunction, and Mr. Flanz is just sitting there, waiting for us, like he's a flunky for Interfor ..."

"Mrs. Krawczyk, please sit down."

"And you, sir, you released Interfor from any responsibility for the costs of this trial. By criminalizing these entire proceedings, Interfor pays for nothing and the taxpayers of British Columbia have been ripped off again. Interfor not only steals away the people's forests, they steal the taxpayers' money, too ..."

I pause for breath.

"Are you quite finished, Mrs. Krawczyk?"

"No, sir. I want to talk about the grounds on which I will be defending myself in my new trial with Miss Jackson."

"This is not the time for that, Mrs. Krawczyk. You may do that at the appropriate time. And I will not be the judge for your new trial."

Well, that's a relief. I sit down. One trial under Mr. Justice Parrett is quite enough. And I think he is relieved that I have decided to sit down rather than follow Suzanne. The judge pours himself a glass of water from the pitcher on his desk. My eye is drawn to the pitcher. Odd, I hadn't noticed before that the judge has a fancier pitcher than the defence lawyers and Crown counsel. I, of course, sitting in the prisoner's box, have no pitcher at all, even though I am defending myself and get just as thirsty as the other players in this courtroom game.

And I am convinced this is a game, a disgusting game, because it is heavily stacked in favour of the international logging companies operating in British Columbia. The judicial system of the province acts as a built-in protective hard-drive for the logging companies, ensuring their interests are safe-guarded. This became clear to me, as well as to many others, back in 1993 during the Clayoquot Sound trials. At that time I was living in Clayoquot Sound on the west coast of Vancouver Island, and was among the first dozen people arrested for blockading logging trucks entering the area. Before that summer was over, nearly nine hundred people were arrested in their efforts to save the magnificent beauty and biodiversity of Clayoquot Sound, on the west coast of Vancouver Island.

That was my very first arrest. The experience was a real eye-opener. I learned then how the logging companies are protected by the courts and the provincial government against any significant action by citizens concerned about the trashing of public forests. The procedure under which we are arrested and charged predicts the outcome of our trials.

Canadian citizens are protected by the Criminal Code and the Charter of Rights and Freedoms. If anti-logging protesters were treated like all other citizens, we would be arrested and charged under the Criminal Code, which makes provisions for an accused's defence. The reasons for the crime and the circumstances surrounding the crime would then be taken into account by a judge or jury. We would be able to bring into the public consciousness the fact that logging corporations are stealing the forests that belong to us and our children and grandchildren. Instead, an unholy threesome—corporate companies like Interfor, the Attorney General's office and the judiciary—circumvents justice in the province of British Columbia by refusing protesters the protections of the Criminal Code. They do this by arresting us under an injunction.

It works like this: If one or two or ten or a hundred people decide to exercise a little participatory democracy and try to protect a particular forest for future generations by standing in the middle of a logging road or interfering in any way with corporate destruction of our forests, all the logging company needs to know is the name of one of the people involved. Just one. Then they go to court, sue this one person and ask for an injunction, which is a restraining order. The beauty of this kind of largesse from the courts is that the judge will tack an "et al" after the accused person's name, meaning that anyone—and this could mean the entire population of North America—is forbidden to go into the area where the company in question is logging. Any trespasser caught blocking a road or swinging from a tree or simply being in the area will be charged with contempt of court. And once he or she is charged, the transformation of civil contempt of court into criminal contempt of court is plumb astonishing.

Judges have ruled in the past that a charge of civil contempt changes to criminal contempt based on how public the protest is. In 1992 Chief Justice Beverley McLachlin ruled that when a person not only breaches a court order but publicly defies the court's process in a way calculated to lessen societal respect for the court, the charge is criminal contempt of court. Since attracting public attention (and hopefully support for one's cause) is one of the main reasons for civil disobedience, the citizen who decides to put his or her body on the line is almost certain to be charged with criminal contempt of court. But when a charge is elevated to criminal contempt, this doesn't mean that you will then have the protection of the Criminal Code. Oh, no. All it means is that your punishment will be harsher. It is still contempt of court, so the provisions of the Criminal Code don't apply. In other words, a murderer can have his or her reasons for murdering someone taken into account by a judge, but an antilogging protester does not have that right.

I wrote Madam Chief Justice and told her of my disappointment in learning that she comes down so hard on civil disobedience. I told her that if it had not been for all those gutsy women who preceded her and indulged in civil disobedience, she would not be Chief Justice of Canada. She would not be a judge or even a lawyer; she would be at home darning her husband's socks.

I blocked that road at Mile 21 in the Elaho for two whole days before I was arrested on the third morning. And even though I was breaking the law and I talked to RCMP officers numerous times during those days, I wasn't arrested until Interfor gave the word to arrest me. The police, in fact, take orders from the logging companies on instruction from the Attorney General's office. I had learned that back in 1993 during the Clayoquot trials.

And I paid for my lesson with four months of my life. That's how long I was in prison for my crimes in Clayoquot Sound. Most of that time I could have been free had I been willing to sign a document promising not to return to the area where I was arrested. But my legal and moral stance was the same then as it is now. If one truly believes, as I do, that the public forests of British Columbia belong to the people of British Columbia, then signing a document that says I have no business protesting the destruction of my own forests doesn't sit right with me. I contend that I have every right to protest the clearcut logging of these ancient forests that belong to all of us. So I refused to sign this piece of paper, called an undertaking. It's deplorable that seven years after the Clayoquot blockades—the largest act of civil disobedience in Canadian history, one that culminated in the arrests of 856 people—the provincial government refuses to publicly address this fundamental question: To whom do our public forests belong? To the public, or to the corporate logging corporations? I say they belong to me, to the citizens of British Columbia, to Canadians. So I have thrown down the gauntlet. There's no alternative now but to hang tough.

I had just moved to Vancouver from Victoria to live with my youngest daughter Marian when the simmering tensions in the Elaho suddenly erupted into violence. The Elaho Valley is located northeast of Squamish, some 200 kilometres northwest of Vancouver. Since 1997 environmental groups have used various strategies to stop the logging of old-growth Douglas fir and to pressure the Government of Canada to designate the Stoltmann Wilderness area in the Elaho as a national park. On September 15, 1999, a mob of Interfor employees and their friends attacked a camp of peaceful young people who were monitoring logging procedures. There were seven men in the camp and one woman. Some say fifty, some say sixty, some say eighty or ninety loggers and their cohorts participated in the attack. The people in the camp were kicked and beaten and their belongings were burned. Three of the young people, including the woman, were sent to hospital.

When I heard about the attack, my gut churned with outrage. How could this happen? Surely the management of Interfor knew this was coming down the pike. How dare this company make British Columbia look like a Third World dictatorship with roving goon squads? The whole business sat on my chest in the days that followed. I couldn't eat or sleep. I had to do something. Finally I made a decision. I would go to the Elaho myself.

So two weeks after Interfor employees and their associates brutally attacked the camp of concerned citizens, I found myself blockading the main logging road into the Elaho Valley. Friends and supporters stood by me, but they moved off the road when the RCMP arrived. I was the only one standing for arrest on that blockade.

It took two days for Interfor to decide to have me arrested. For this little while a wild, enchanted forest that shelters streams, waterfalls, glaciers and a large stand of some of the oldest Douglas fir trees in the world had a brief reprieve from the carnage of Interfor's clearcutting. An old-growth forest close enough to Vancouver that a family can arrive in the morning, spend the day and return by nightfall, was protected for a few more days. That thought comforted me somewhat as I was hauled off to jail.

I was by no means the only concerned citizen arrested in the Elaho. Twelve others had gone before me. They had already established an Elaho account, so to speak, with Mr. Justice Parrett. And although we were arrested on different days, for different actions, we are all being tried together. The thirteen of us can be treated as one under contempt of court rules, so when one of us as an individual gets charged with criminal contempt of court, then the entire trial becomes criminalized. And then the Attorney General's office takes over as prosecutor. Barney Kern, a thirty-five-year-old environmentalist, and I have been charged with criminal contempt of court. Barney was one of the first to discover what Interfor was doing to the Elaho Valley. He was able to help spread the news around, get together a few dollars and a few bodies to try to bring the situation to public attention.

Now eight of us are in court this morning before Mr. Justice Parrett. Four of our co-accused pleaded guilty to civil contempt and are no longer connected with this trial; one other person who was charged has left the country. We are here primarily to learn when the trial, which has been recessed for weeks because of a technicality with one of the Crown's witnesses, will resume. But Suzanne and I are also here to learn when we will be tried on our new charges.

And I fault Mr. Justice Parrett for his role in these new charges. If he hadn't kept asking me to sign an undertaking of some sort to get out of jail while the original trial was going on, I wouldn't be in this predicament: facing two separate charges of contempt of court. He asked me at least half a dozen times to sign a promise not to return to the Elaho, which I refused. But then he came up with a proposition I found hard to refuse. I wouldn't be asked not to go back to the Elaho, only to keep the peace. Well, it was getting close to Christmas. I signed the document and was released.

Which was a mistake. I knew, and I think Mr. Justice Parrett knew, that my idea of peace and his idea of peace were remarkably different. And with the spring came increased logging in the Elaho. So on May 15, 2000, I peacefully flung myself down in the middle of the same Elaho logging road where I was arrested before. Only this time Suzanne Jackson locked arms with me and we shared the ride to the Squamish police station. And we both refused to sign the infernal undertaking. Which meant that we were both immediately packed off to the women's prison in Burnaby.

Where we still reside. At least for the foreseeable future. Meanwhile nobody in the mob that criminally attacked peaceful citizens has been charged with anything. But I won't let myself get bitter. I have to keep my mind on what is happening here. Mr. Justice Parrett is simmering like a pot of Louisiana hot sauce. I have disobeyed his orders and refused his authority. I am a foolish old woman who needs to be taught a lesson. Maybe the judge is just a mean ole man. Not old man, because he isn't that old; in fact, despite a streak of grey hair, he moves like a young man, and he's certainly many years my junior. Maybe the bench just attracts mean ole men, though I know there are some women judges out there somewhere.

The tension is rising.

But David Haffey is not present, so the trial cannot proceed. Mr. Haffey is a witness for the Crown who has proved to be a potential ace in the hole for us, the accused. Mr. Haffey, an employee at Interfor, admitted on the stand to videotaping the attack of September 15, 1999—the attack that sent three protesters to the hospital. He broke down on the witness stand under cross-examination, admitted that he had tossed the tape over the Lava Creek bridge under threat by his co-workers, then changed his story and said no, there had been no threat, he had tossed the tape of his own volition. At which point he broke down entirely and went home in need of immediate care by health professionals. He couldn't come back to court, his lawyer said, so the court disbanded until today. Still no Mr. Haffey.

But I am tired of Mr. Haffey. The judge has already told us that whatever happened on September 15 at the protest camp won't affect the outcome of our trial. So why is the court spending so much time on this? I feel like yelling that this trial is supposed to be about what we eight people did in the Elaho, not what the unfortunate Mr. Haffey did, or what happened to the damn tape. This trial is supposed to be about justice, but there isn't any because there is no legal defence for criminal contempt of court, of which we are all accused, and it annoys me no end that any judge, especially this one, pretends that there is. But to be fair, Mr. Justice Parrett admits he is only interested in one thing: Did we or did we not break his injunction? Which is another legal point to which I take exception. Judges have a tendency to defend other judges' injunctions on general principle, but when it comes to their own, well, they can wax plumb emotional. Every jit and jot of the order is their very own; how could they possibly be objective about disobedience of it? Protesters should never be brought for trial before the same judge who issued an injunction. However, this seems to be acceptable practice in British Columbia.

The court day lumbers on. By four o'clock Suzanne and I have a trial date for our charges stemming from our two-woman song-and-dance road show performed at Mile 21 on May 15, 2000, on the Squamish Valley Road in the Elaho Valley. We sang and danced and blocked about thirty logging trucks for a little while. Our trial for that performance will start on June 5, and my original trial under Mr. Justice Parrett with the seven other co-accused will resume on June 26. Oh, busy, busy, busy.

By the time court is over, I feel exhausted. But the best is yet to come. Oh, yes, the ride back to BCCW. Suzanne and I are searched, handcuffed, leg-ironed and escorted into the back of the sheriff's paddy wagon along with five other women. I glance at Suzanne. She looks wan. Her rounded, lovely face is almost as pale as her flaxen hair. She is only twenty-two. She is tall and slender and in her freshness exudes the greenness of the forest. But underneath all that youthful, innocent freshness, Suzanne Jackson is busy forging a spine of steel.

After we are settled, four male prisoners are brought into the front section of the wagon. The sexes are separated by rigid plastic sheeting that has steel wire woven in between the sheets, but the men and women can see each other. Some of them know each other, and immediately a lively exchange ensues about drugs, East Hastings Street, fights, who is whose old lady or old man. One of the women is drug sick and upchucks right at my feet. Suzanne and I try to scrunch over but there is no place to scrunch to. We are packed in. I am happy to arrive back at our stark, but clean, prison.

When I first embarked upon a life of crime back in 1993, I didn't understand why we grandmothers (there were two other grandmother protesters with me at the time) were put in the maximum security section. It was explained that all new inmates go there first. One must be assessed. Is one suicidal? Violent? Crazy? Prone to escape? After a few days, weeks, months, even, after thorough assessments, and if one has been sentenced, then one might be considered for the open living unit.

After we consume our frozen dinners, Suzanne and I head for the telephones, she to advise and receive advice from our support groups, I to talk to my daughter Marian. Marian and I live together. She is thirty years old, my youngest of eight. She studies social anthropology at the university and works for Save the Children, an organization concerned with youngsters who are sexually exploited by adults. More bluntly, the organization is concerned with kids who are sold for sexual purposes, usually on the street, to men with deep pockets.

Marian supports herself, but a few years back we couldn't decide which one of us should leave home, so we just stayed living together. We are interested in similar issues and can help each other. Marian labours to save the children, I to save the forests. Neither one of us is getting very far with our saving efforts, and intermittently one or the other bogs down. At the moment she is depressed over the sheer volume of her work and I'm in jail. But one must lock into the struggle. There is no alternative.

There are only two local phones in our unit at BCCW. There are also two long-distance phones on opposite sides of the common room. Suzanne races to one side, I stake out the other. Our unit is what is known as a receiving unit and we are double-bunked. There are thirty women crowded into a space built to house half that number. Is it because of the Chinese boat women that we are double-bunked? Nobody knows for sure. But as usual, I have to wait for the phone. I take a chair by the open, recessed booth to indicate that I'm next. Morning Star (I will refer to all the inmates by beautiful fictitious names) is on the phone now, yelling at her abusive addict of a boyfriend who must also, I gather from her conversation, be her pimp. I try not to listen, but privacy is impossible.

"You son of a bitch, you better bring me some money! I was out on the street selling my pussy for you to suck up your nose and now I'm in here and you can't bring me any fucking money, you shit-head?"

She is silent for a moment. Shit-head is obviously offering excuses. But Morning Star isn't buying them, whatever they are.

"Fuck that! Fuck that, you asshole!" Morning Star yells again. "You're a fucking liar—"

"Morning Star!" a female voice admonishes. I look around. A uniformed officer, alias staff, screw, big bitch, has appeared from nowhere. "You watch your mouth!"

Morning Star blinks, puts her hand over the receiver. "Oh … sorry. I'm sorry," she says to the officer. She looks crestfallen, like a little girl. She's exactly nineteen. Her skin is still smooth, her hair glossy, she still has all of her teeth. If she stays addicted to crack cocaine, if she stays alive, within a few years she will look twice her age, with track marks scarring arms and legs and even her neck. Her face will collapse as the skin withers and her teeth rot. For some reason, the front teeth seem to go first. The drugs are more vicious now, I am told, and the women are addicted much younger, as men demand ever younger, less diseased prostitutes. Morning Star continues to rail at her significant other for a couple of minutes and then, abruptly, she is crying. Her voice has changed from a battle cry into that of a placating lover.

"Oh, honey, I know you're trying," she sobs softly into the phone. "I don't want to be mean to you. Yes, I love you …"

I get up and move away. I'll make my call later. I can't stand it, how these women, some hardly out of girlhood, prostrate themselves before men who endlessly abuse them, seduce them, addict them, beat them, prostitute them and then throw them to the wolves, to the vultures, to the trash heap of humanity. But after a few minutes Morning Star unglues from the phone, motions to me that she is finished. I take my turn.

Marian answers the phone. She was in court this morning, she wants to know about Suzanne and when our new trial will be. I fill her in with what I know. Moving right along in conversation—because we've learned to impart necessary information first and save the stuff about relationships and sheer gossip until last—she tells me about the report she is writing and I give her messages for my other children. And then there is a wrinkle in her romantic relationship that is bothering her and she wants to run it by me. I try to give her the benefit of my long years of experience.

"Honey, listen," I begin. "Listen to your mother's advice—"

"No, Mom, wait a minute," she answers quickly, cutting me off. "I don't want advice. I was just thinking out loud. Anyway, would you take advice from someone locked up in a maximum security prison?"

She's being funny. I laugh. But just a little. Because it does irk me somewhat that not one of my five daughters comes to me for advice on sexual relationships. They will report once in a while, but not actually ask for advice. But why would we, they ask, when you've been married four times? That reply might silence a more thin-skinned woman, but I refuse to be intimidated. "Don't you think that makes me kind of an expert?" I answer. "Why would you ask someone for advice on men and marriage if she had only done it once?" Anyway, I haven't been married to anybody for at least twenty-five years.

But other women are waiting in line for the phone. I give it up graciously. Our calls finished, showers taken, court papers, toilet articles and personal belongings all piled in a jumble on the one built-in corner desk in our tiny cell, Suzanne and I prepare for bed. She pulls her plastic-covered mattress out from underneath my bunk, the only bunk in the room, and positions it on the floor between the desk, the door, the toilet and the sink. It's awful. Suzanne has to sleep with her head either under the desk or disgustingly close to the toilet bowl.

Finally we are settled. An officer comes around and locks us down. I no longer panic at cramped spaces and locked iron doors. I faced that down long ago, back during the Clayoquot imprisonments. And Suzanne is a remarkably stoic young person. She doesn't seem unduly disturbed by any of the prison commotion. "Goodnight," I say. "I was proud to be associated with you today." She murmurs something; she is already half asleep under the soft glare of the light above our heads. This light never goes off. It is the eye of the prison, the ever-watchful eye of maximum security, the gaze of authority.

I can't sleep. It isn't the light, I'm just too hyped up from the day. I need to talk to my mother. I've talked to her all of my life, down through the years, calling to her from another room in the old farmhouse of a million years ago, later calling her from across town in Baton Rouge, still later calling long distance from Virginia, years and years later from Ontario, then British Columbia. Waiting for her voice to answer. Mama, are you there?

But Mama isn't there anymore. She died two years ago, on my seventieth birthday. She was ninety-five. She was frying catfish for Carter, my brother-in-law. The last thing she saw on this earth was a stove and a pan of frying catfish. How fitting. She loved cooking. She loved her relatives. She knew how to lose and start over, let go and face defeat. Yes, give me a woman who knows how to face defeat, count her losses and start over. How to give sway to the loss of parents, siblings, a husband, a daughter. You dig in, close ranks, count your blessings, come out swinging.

Mama, can you hear me, I ask the ever-present light that is making a glossy white-blonde puddle of Suzanne's hair spilled across her mattress on the floor, poor child. Mama, is Barbara Ellen with you? Oh, Mama, how I miss you! Two years? Has it been two years since I last saw you, told you goodbye?

When Mama called me that day in June two years ago and told me to come home, that she needed me, I didn't hesitate. I caught the first plane out.

"I'm coming, Mama," I said. "I'm on my way."

Chapter Two

Mama was so upset when she phoned that I expected to find Aunt Gladys, Mama's younger sister, either dead or near death when I arrived in Vicksburg, Mississippi. However, by the time I got there, Aunt Gladys had survived her heart attack and was on top of things as usual, though she was still in the hospital.

Mama had lived in my sister's house in Baton Rouge for forty years, but on a visit to Vicksburg several years ago she had fallen into Aunt Gladys' clutches again. At ninety-five, Mama was still robust. Aunt Gladys, at ninety, had taken to her bed, more or less, and expected Mama to wait on her. How could a ninety-five-year-old woman be a nurse? But it seemed to work, after a fashion. Aunt Gladys wasn't exactly housebound. A visiting nurse came in every other day for an hour or so, and there was a cleaning lady. I spent several months with Mama and Aunt Gladys each year. So did my brother Ray Allen and his wife Carol. But it still ground my gizzard that Aunt Gladys monopolized Mama's attention. Aunt Gladys looked upon me not as her niece, but as a rival for Mama's affection. So we were ancient enemies, Aunt Gladys and I.

Not that I would have liked Aunt Gladys under any circumstances. When she was young, she ruled with her vivacious dark beauty; later she ruled men and family members with the money she made in her restaurants. In her extreme old age Aunt Gladys lacked beauty, men and money, but she did have Mama—much to my disgust. I hated seeing Mama dancing attendance on Aunt Gladys' every whim.

Back in Baton Rouge, Mama had her own apartment in a big house on the edge of one of the oldest, most gracious neighbourhoods. The house was modest enough on the outside, but it was jazzed up on the inside by my late sister's architect son. On the Louisiana side of the Mississippi River my mother had a son-in-law and grandsons and their wives to wait on her. They loved her and kept her apartment empty in case of her return. But no. Mama chose to go live with Aunt Gladys in a mobile home park way out in the Mississippi boonies. Of course, we were all country people from way back. It just irked me that Aunt Gladys still ruled her older sister through the mechanism of the "tyranny of the weak."

On my second day in Vicksburg I took Mama to the hospital in Aunt Gladys' old Buick. It was Aunt Gladys' third day in the hospital and the nurses were already showing the strain: they seemed inordinately relieved to see us. I felt sure that within their heart of hearts there had been times in the last three days when most would have been happy to place Aunt Gladys on one of those rolling stretchers and run her through the hospital corridors, across the road and down the highway a piece and, with a good hearty shove, sail her right into the Mississippi River. Or maybe I was just projecting.

After greetings, Mama sat by Aunt Gladys' bed, trying to soothe her sister, who was full of complaints about the hospital in general and the food in particular.

"It's just for a few more days, Gladys," Mama said. "And when we get home this evening Betty will make you some chicken and dumplings to bring tomorrow, won't you, Betty?"

They both turned to look at me. These women were incredible cooks. They were professionals. I always felt flattered when they said I cooked something well. And they—Aunt Gladys, too—gave me high marks for my chicken and dumplings.

"Yes, Mama," I agreed. "I'll fix them as soon as we get home."

"Careful you don't scorch them," Aunt Gladys cautioned, fixing me with the look. I hated that look, had from childhood, that look that said *be careful, little girl, I know you, I know what you're really like and I'll tell your mama on you* ...

It's her eyes, I decided as I stood there gazing back at my old auntie, who hardly made a rumple under the sheet, she had become so thin. Cow eyes. Big, brown, boldly appraising, even now in illness and extreme old age. I somehow got locked into our old animosities by the ever-ready challenge in her eyes. And I hated her fingernails. They were long, the same length she had kept them in her femme fatale years. Against the whiteness of the hospital sheets and the pale blue of her wrinkled hands, the bright red talons seemed startling, even frightening. I swallowed a quick retort to my aunt's thinly veiled challenge. I had promised Mama not to quarrel with Aunt Gladys, at least not while she was hospitalized. In any case, at that moment I just wanted the visit to be over so I could get out of the hospital before Sarah Sue came sailing in.

The day before, Sarah Sue had caught me unaware and unprepared. Sarah Sue was a born-again Christian. She and her husband and their two children had once lived in the same mobile home park as my mother and aunt, back in the days when southern whites were fleeing cities and school integration. Integration came more slowly to the countryside, so Sarah Sue's son and daughter were spared actually having to associate with black people on an equal basis in a

27

school situation. That horrible moral catastrophe averted, Sarah Sue and her family promptly moved back to their beautiful home in Vicksburg after the children graduated. Raised in racial purity, the two children went on to study religion and counselling at a Bible college, which made Sarah Sue very proud.

The day before, after filling me in on her children's accomplishments, she had told me that she had read my book about the Clayoquot Sound and was indeed inspired to write one of her own. After all, if I could write a book, certainly she could, only hers would have a more uplifting message, more inspirational, you know. And then she shoved a religious tract into my hand. Today I was prepared. I had with me some copies of choice excerpts from Valerie Solanas' SCUM Manifesto. Just for fun. Just in case.

But no, I was spared. Sarah Sue didn't come. But Mama wanted to stop by the nurses' station on our way out.

"My sister is complaining she can't sleep at night," Mama confided to the nurse behind the large, encircling desk. "I was wondering if you could give her something to help her sleep."

The middle-aged nurse nodded and reached up with some difficulty to take a chart off the wall. She was extremely wide through the beam and somewhat breathless after the exertion of reaching for the clipboard. She shuffled through some papers clipped to the chart. "Ummmm," she said thoughtfully, and then looked at Mama over the counter. "Ma'am, your sister is already getting sleeping medicine." Mama leaned over the counter in a conspiratorial manner, motioning to the nurse to step closer. The nurse complied.

"You reckon you could make it a mite stronger?" Mama asked in the low, firm tone she uses when she means business. "Gladys calls, you see. On the telephone. Late at night."

"She means the morning," I interjected. "Anywhere from midnight to four o'clock in the morning."

The nurse nodded understandingly. "We can't have that now, can we? I'll talk to her doctor. Don't you worry none, Mrs. Shiver."

Mama had that effect on people. She was old, but her smile was so sweet, her hair so white, her manner so winsome, her clothes so well made because she made them herself, that she fairly radiated intelligence and good will. Mama thanked the nurse graciously and we made our way down the hall to the elevators that led to the parking lot.

Southern Mississippi lies just across the Mississippi River from southern Louisiana, and both lie just this side of hell. Hell is situated that close by so that Mississippi and Louisiana people, being already conditioned, both morally and physically, to hellish conditions, can just slide right into the great inferno without much ado, especially during June, July and August.

When I went to fetch Aunt Gladys' old Buick from the parking lot, I thought I might faint before I got the car door open. However, I managed to slide into the front seat and turn on the air conditioning. It took the old buggy a few minutes to kick in so I waited, wanting it to be reasonably cool when I went back to the entrance to pick up Mama. That's when I glanced up and saw the dark-haired young woman walking briskly through the wet heat toward the hospital entrance. I stared after her for a moment, tensing, trying to head off the emotional ambush that occurred every time I saw a young woman who reminded me of my daughter Barbara Ellen.

Barbara Ellen had died two years before, of breast cancer. I was still very raw from the loss. She had left behind a little boy who lived with his daddy in Victoria. How could a healthy twenty-seven-year-old woman die from breast cancer? Breast cancer was an elder woman's disease, and here was Mama, in her mid-nineties, me hitting the elder stride, pushing seventy, and yet it was my young daughter ... It didn't make sense. It made no sense at all. And there was Andy, my son ...

It took effort to bring my mind back, away from Andy, my youngest son. He was doing well. I had to be thankful for that. He wouldn't die, not like Barbara Ellen did. Andy had taken a different tack: he had a different attitude, he went for whatever medical science had to offer, he would accept the knife if it came to that, the chemo, the radiation, the works, he would take it and come back for more, but it was okay now, he was steadily improving. Put down those thoughts of self-pity; mothers have suffered worse, mothers have seen all their children die from hunger, die in wars, die on the highways, die from guns. I am not unique; the gods are not singling me out for special torment. But how could cancer strike two of my eight children—not one, but two. Is there no mercy or justice anywhere?

The young woman making her way to the hospital entrance did not, on second glance, look much like Barbara Ellen. Barbara Ellen's hair was darker, and she had walked like a dancer, which is what she had trained to be. Working in her little ballet studio in Ucluelet, on the west coast of British Columbia, she had wanted to choreograph a ballet that included Native myth and Native dance. She wanted to try to take dance away from the classical norm that dictated dancers be skin and bone, she wanted ... oh, so many things. But I must get this junk of a car around to the front entrance of the hospital where Mama is waiting.

Mama was sitting on a chair right by the door inside the air-conditioned hospital. Something was wrong with the Buick's air conditioning, but Mama was so worried about Aunt Gladys she hardly seemed to notice that it was almost as hot inside the car as out. But we made it home without mishap, and soon Mama was resting in her chair in her bedroom under her own little air conditioner with a tall glass of iced tea. I made a trip down to the corner country store, which just happened to have a plump, juicy hen. Just what I needed for dumplings.

Banish all nagging worries from my head: Marian, trying to finish up the last semester of her second year of university in my tiny bachelorette senior's apartment (where she isn't supposed to be living); Andy, struggling with the big C; Julian, Barbara Ellen's little boy, who is always on my mind; Aunt Gladys' declining health, which means that Mama will soon have to be relocated; the struggling little group of women called The Canadian Party of Women, which Jannit Rabinovich and I were helping to organize in Victoria. Yes, banish it all, there is nothing in the universe at the moment but the plump hen cooked until tender, big glass bowl, four heaping cups of flour, make plenty for dinner, too, baking powder, salt, tiny dash of sugar (just for luck), pour in the hot juice, enough to make a big ball of dough, handle lightly, roll out quickly with deft, even strokes, cut into thin strips, very thin strips, ah, very nice, just the right consistency, and then tenderly lower the strips, one by one, into the ever-so-gently bubbling chicken juice.

As the last dumpling strip hit the pot there was a knock at the door. It was Sonny. He and his wife Geraldine own the mobile home park. He was fixing an outside faucet and needed to use the phone. I asked him in. Sonny was a big talker. By the time I had brought him up to date on Aunt Gladys' condition and Mama's state of being, and he had explained in detail the problem with the outside faucet, I had to remind him to make his call. Sonny, unlike most Southern men in their fifties, didn't have a noticeable paunch. But he could talk the horns off a billy goat. Just like my father. I grew up with Daddy's voice in my ear and learned early to tune him out, but I couldn't tune Sonny out. I had to wait until he was actually out the door before I could turn my whole attention back to the dumplings.

Just in time, too. I stirred quickly. There was only the tiniest speck of brown on the bottom of one dumpling. I could hardly see it. Nevertheless, I checked the centre of the bottom of the pot just to be sure. No, no taste of scorch. And at dinner, Mama pronounced the dumplings perfect. After the dishes were done I encouraged Mama to go back to her room. The air conditioner there was new and vigorous while the one in the living and dining area was threatening, like the Buick's air conditioner, to expire. I had taken the front grille off before we went to the hospital and peered inside. I knew absolutely nothing about air conditioners but I could tell—anybody could tell—that the thing was teetering on some kind of mechanical rot. And as we were in the midst of a heat wave in one of the hottest places on earth, naturally no air-conditioning repair person could be found. Well, it was too late to call anybody now. I filled a tall glass with iced tea and went out on the front screened porch to see if there was an evening breeze.

There was. I sat amid the three fans, four easy chairs and the telephone. Southerners used to be great ones for porch sitting but nobody much sat out on their porches anymore. Everybody had air conditioning and TV inside. And even the elders, who preferred the porch, couldn't indulge without risking heat stroke. It was simply hotter than it used to be. Statistically hotter. And dryer. Southern Louisiana was in a drought mode, dragging parts of southern Mississippi along with it. Whoever heard of a drought in southern Louisiana? Why, southern Louisiana, before all the logging and development, was a rainforest. The entire area had become hotter and dryer because of the loss of the climate-moderating wetlands, the wetlands I knew as a child.

In Louisiana where I was raised, out from Baton Rouge, I no longer even liked driving what used to be the old Hammond Highway or the country roads that led down toward the swamps that were no longer there. The moss-hung trees had all been cut, the swamps drained, the very ghosts of my childhood had long ago departed, along with the wild animals and birds I took for granted. Is Louisiana still the pelican state? How can that be, without pelicans? Where have all the wild geese gone, the long interconnecting bayous, the alligators, the wild cats, the sweet clean streams full of catfish and perch and flounder, the side ditches full of crayfish just for the swoopin' ... Where did it all go? Did we eat it, did we consume it, did we burn it, did we kill it?

At least the cicadas were still coming back. The mobile home park was cut out of a woodland and the cicadas were just starting to gear up for the night. These critters only come once every seven years. So odd, when I thought of it. The locust's eggs fall to the ground at the end of the summer and burrow underneath and incubate for seven whole years before a new crop of cicadas appear and begin anew where their ancestors left off. If humans had that cycle, I thought to myself, the earth would be the finer. A seven-year rest between human life cycles. At least that would slow down the destruction of the earth's life support systems. But the cicadas were making the most of their brief appearance on the stage of life. In fact, the entire section of woods surrounding the trailer park was rocking.

Wild. I wished all my kids and grandkids could hear this. The frogs were singing their little throats out along with the crickets and cicadas. How to describe to my family this nightly throbbing of the southern Mississippi woods in summer? Impossible. They would have to come hear it themselves. Marian had been down several times for extended visits; Rose Mary came when she was a teenager; Margaret and Andre came on their honeymoon; Sue had visited, too, but none of them had heard the cicadas. Oh, well. So much of my life was incomprehensible to my children, even the ones who were old enough to remember, the ones who had lived through catastrophic changes with me. Like school integration in the late fifties and early sixties.

The state of Louisiana wasn't exactly progressive in the matter. Some schools in New Orleans closed rather than integrate. The integration was beginning in elementary schools when my youngest son Andy was school age. Would our schools in Baton Rouge close, too, rather than allow black kids to attend? What a revolting development that would be. I went down and demonstrated in front of our school along with a handful of other white people who were demanding that our schools stay open and integrate peacefully. And I was promptly rewarded for my efforts with condemnation and even outright ostracism by neighbours, friends, my church, and even some members of my family. Hate mail. Garbage in our front yard. But I think what hurt me the most was that Christian principles could not overcome hate and prejudice.

Everybody I knew was a Christian. The church was the centre of our social life. Under the social pressures of school integration I began to pull away from the church, first because I doubted that religion could stand up to the moral issues of the day, and second, because I came to question church doctrine in its entirety. My mother was searching for ways to support me in my stand on integration during this time, but she reacted with alarm when I voiced disgust with the church and with Christianity itself.

"Betty, you can't throw over God and Jesus Christ because people are imperfect," she said one afternoon when she had come to babysit the little ones so I could go grocery shopping.

"But why not?" I answered. "If Christianity doesn't work, if there is no practical application for it in a situation like this where white Christian people can use the Bible to excuse oppressing black people, then to heck with it, Mama."

Mama leaned down and picked up Margaret Elizabeth from her crib. The baby gurgled her pleasure at waking to see her grandma.

"Bite your tongue, child," Mama answered, cuddling the baby. "Someday you'll learn that faith is belief in the substance of things unseen."

"You're quoting scripture," I retorted, picking up my purse. This was simply a quick rehash. This conversation between Mama and me had been going on for months.

"Yes. But it's the truth. We don't know really what we're doing here, why we're given all these tests. We can only have faith that something is evolving, that God is with us, even when it seems there is nothing, that our job is simply to do the best we can, every day."

"I know, Mama," I answered impatiently.

She gave me a long, searching look over my baby's blonde, fuzzy head.

"No, you don't," she said firmly. "Betty, if we do the best we can every day, God will take care of the rest. We can't see the future because the future belongs to itself, and to God. You're a Christian, Betty, a real Christian, or trying to be, because you're saying we have to love our coloured neighbours as ourselves, as well as white ones. If you just hold to that, in the long run nobody will be able to refute you because you're following Christ. But if you say you don't believe in God anymore, then what will people say? You know what they'll say? That you're a heathen, so who should listen to you."

"So you want me to lie and say I believe something I don't believe anymore?" I asked, making my way to the door.

There was a long silence.

"No," she said finally. "Of course not. That's the worst thing." Our eyes locked, held. Finally she smiled. "Go. Go do your shopping. You know I'll stand by you, whatever you do."

I quit the church. That's what I did. I explained as best I could to the kids. They seemed to accept my explanations. Poor babies. They've had to accept so much, I thought, sitting there on the porch with the fans whirring and the mosquitoes buzzing and the Missis-sippi woods rocking with myriad insect life. Oh, well. The moving finger having writ, moves on, as the poet said. And it was time to go to bed. The world and all its inhabitants would have to take care of themselves until tomorrow. Only I had hardly closed my eyes for the night when the phone rang in the kitchen. It was Aunt Gladys. I glanced at the clock. It was midnight, straight up.

"Betty, let me speak to Bug," Aunt Gladys demanded without preliminaries.

My mother was called Bug by all who knew her except her children and grandchildren. Evidently back when Mama was born, country people didn't just hop right on to the naming of their kids. In fact, ru-ral kids might go without proper names for years until somebody got around to doing some serious thinking on the matter. So of course nicknames stuck forever, even when formal names were given. Bug was short for Doodle-Bug.

"Aunt Gladys, Mama is asleep," I said firmly.

"Well, wake her up. I have to talk to her."

"No," I answered, more firmly than before. "Mama's tired. She's worn out from coming to see you and then you don't let her sleep at night. Just tell me what you want her to know and I'll tell her in the morning."

Why in the hell couldn't the hospital get Aunt Gladys' medicine right, I wondered. And whoever started putting telephones in patients' rooms anyway? Weren't sick people supposed to rest instead of talking on the damn phone? I thought perhaps I would just hang up and unplug the phone until morning. That would work. But before I could carry out the plan, Mama appeared in the doorway.

"Who is it?" she asked, blinking against the kitchen light. "Is it Gladys? Is she all right?"

I still could have said it was a wrong number and hung up and unplugged the phone, since Mama didn't have her glasses on, but she looked so small and defenceless standing there in her printed cotton pyjamas. In her prime Mama had been a middling-sized woman, somewhat taller than my father. I couldn't try to play tricks on her in her old age for any reason, so I admitted it was Aunt Gladys on the line and gave over the phone to her. But I hung onto the counter next to Mama, just to hear what Aunt Gladys had to say.

"Bug, the aliens are here," Aunt Gladys said clearly. Aliens? "They're taking over the hospital," she went on in a shrill, excited voice. "One of them was just in here talking to me."

Wow. The promised increase in medication might not be rocking

Aunt Gladys to sleep but at least it was providing more interesting topics of conversation.

"Whatever are you talking about, Gladys?" Mama asked in an aggravated tone.

"Bug, listen ... I'm telling you the God's truth. One of them aliens was just in my room, a little fella with a big head. And he had these round, bulging eyes. He told me there were hundreds of aliens in the hospital just like him. He said they've come to take over. Bug, I want you and Betty to come get me, right now!"

Mama was silent for a long moment.

"Bug, you and Betty come get me right this minute!"

Aunt Gladys' shrieking command ricocheted through the little kitchenette with the frilly blue curtains and the little girl geese herder dressed in matching blue who marched plump white geese with blue ribbons tied around their necks across the wall over to the closed window, where the varied night sounds of the cicadas and the crickets and the katydids and the frogs could be heard ever so faintly above the hum of the barely working air conditioner. I eagerly awaited Mama's answer to this unexpected challenge. But she was not to be hurried. She was thinking.

"Bug!" Aunt Gladys screamed.

"Gladys, just calm down," Mama said calmly. "And stop yelling—"

"But these aliens—"

"All right, tell me about them. Are they friendly?"

"What ... what do you mean?"

"Did this little fella ... the one that was in your room, did he threaten you in any way?"

"Threaten me? No, but they're taking over the hospital!"

"Well, let's see now," Mama went on calmly. "You're always complaining about the hospital, about the food and how slow the nurses are. What if these aliens, these little people, can do things better? You know, maybe that's what they came down here for. They probably want to make a lot of improvements so folks will get well faster. And they probably know how to cook. You remember just the other day the governor was saying the hospitals needed to be rejuvenated. Maybe the governor sent the aliens. I think you ought to at least give the little people a chance. You know, out of respect for the governor, if nothing else."

I tried to stifle a gasp. Why, the woman was brilliant! I felt a thrill of pride in our kinship. But the silence on the other end of the phone was growing long. Was Aunt Gladys buying it?

"Well ... maybe you're right, Bug. Maybe I ought to at least give the little buggers a chance."

Mama and I breathed a collective sigh of relief. Oh, Mama was so smart about most things! That's why I miss talking to her so much now, in this maximum security prison where I am locked up and down with thirty women in various stages of acute distress. If she were still alive, she could help me figure things out the way she always did. We all need someone who has walked before us, who can point out the mud holes, the bend where wild, hungry beasts attack, the fork in the road where one can be set upon by vicious savages. Now there is no one before me who has swum the murky waters, waded through the snake-infested bog.

For the first time in my life I must make all of my life decisions alone, without my mother's counsel. Without her pointing out the other side of everything. Like the Vietnam War. Oh, how we fought over that one! Not that Mama agreed with the American military in-volvement—she didn't. But she was horrified when she learned that I was planning to move to Canada with my family.

"But I can't stand it, Mama," I cried that day when Mama and I were in her kitchen fixing dinner for my brood. My husband John was working for NASA and we were living in Virginia at the time, but we wanted to be in Canada by the end of the month, so we had come to Baton Rouge to tell our parents and siblings goodbye. We were leaving more than family. We had a lovely home in Virginia, an old farmhouse sitting on eighty acres. Our front lawn rolled right down to an inlet of the Chesapeake Bay. John had the job of his dreams as a research physicist and the kids were all settled in their respective schools.

But this happy state of affairs was suddenly interrupted when Joey, our oldest, dropped out of university and joined the Air Force. At that point I began to realize that we had so much because others had so little, and that this unfair allocation of resources was kept in place by force, by the American military, by the bodies of American boys when the situation demanded it.

"Betty, you and John and your kids are American. You can't just switch countries. I know things are rotten here right now, but you should stay here and fight this thing as an American, the way you've been doing."

"No, Mama. It's not worth it. There's Mike. He's next in line. You want to see him come home in a body bag?"

Mama paused in her cornbread preparation. She didn't beat corn-bread batter, she folded it. When it came out of the oven it was crispy brown on the outside, and firm and evenly textured on the inside.

"Don't be crazy," she snapped. "A lot of boys are refusing to join up. They're going to prison instead."

"And they're getting five years—five years of being branded cowards and getting beat up in prison. You know how Mike is about the outdoors, Mama. He'd die in prison."

"Betty, all I know is this one thing," she said, pausing to slide the cornbread pan into the oven. Mama always heated the pan before she poured in the batter. She shut the oven door and turned to me, her mouth set in a firm line. "You have to fight on your own home ground," she continued. "You have to fight where God put you."

"I don't believe in God, Mama. And I didn't raise my sons to go over to some poor little ole foreign country and kill people or be killed by them. Joey is safe for the moment. He's in a communications unit stationed in Italy. But the American military still has him, they stole him when I wasn't looking and they will get another of my sons literally over my dead body."

"All right. I understand the way you're thinking. But I don't agree with it. And you may have trashed God and the Saviour but I know you try to find what's right. And so will your kids if you give them a chance. God put you here, in this country. If you go off to Canada, who will you turn to when things go bad? All your folks are here. Your blood is here, your history. You'll cut your kids adrift and they won't know where they belong and neither will you. Work through it from here."

"You work through it from here, Mama. I'm going to Canada and I'm taking my husband and kids with me."

And I did. But Mama was right about being around kinfolk. When things went bad between me and John, when our marriage crumbled under the strains of relocation, there weren't any home folks to turn to. What John and I turned to was the divorce court.

Okay, Mama, so you could see further than I, I concede into the night at the Burnaby Correctional Centre for Women. And I was so afraid of going to jail back then! What a laugh. I'm practically making being in jail a career at this point in my life. But I have to think, think about how I'm going to prepare myself psychologically for when Suzanne and I have to return for our trial in the criminal court of British Columbia. We have two weeks to prepare ourselves.

Chapter Three

We lucked out this time. Suzanne and I drew Madam Justice Gill for our separate trial, the trial where we face charges stemming from our actions of May 15, 2000, when we locked arms and were arrested together. It is my second offence for blockading in the Elaho, Suzanne's first.

Madam Justice Gill doesn't seem to know much about the situation in the Elaho, but she listens attentively. On the whole, she asks intelligent, unbiased questions in a reasonable voice, devoid of sarcasm. She seems to take Suzanne's application to be tried before the Squamish people seriously, and she smiles once in a while.

Best of all, Madam Justice Gill lets me rant and rave about the damn injunctions and why they are discriminatory and prejudicial and how they seem to be reserved primarily for anti-logging protesters. Robert Moore-Stewart, Suzanne's lawyer, puts her on the stand and Suzanne talks about her love and concern for the forest and the forest animals in such a knowledgeable and straightforward way I can tell Madam Justice Gill is impressed. And I feel sure, at least on some level, that Madam is concerned about Suzanne's hunger strike. Suzanne, naturally slender to start with, is in the ninth day of a hunger strike and might be in danger of starving to death. The thought is scary to all of us, including Crown Counsel.

So that trial goes okay. Suzanne gets out with time served, and

I draw an additional six weeks. Which isn't all that bad, considering. So I go back to Burnaby Correctional Centre for Women to await the resumption of the original trial under Mr. Justice Parrett.

⋅

It has now been a little over a month since I was in the courtroom with the mean ole man, and today is the day to return. Just the process of getting to court from BCWW is an ordeal in itself. I am awakened at five-thirty by the guard unlocking my door. The next few hours will be miserable, but I'm happy just to be awake. My sleep, what there was of it, was nightmare-ridden.

I dreamed the judge was holding me in a death grip with one arm and he wanted to murder me. I was trying to struggle, but his grasp was like iron. He was holding an old-fashioned razor in his free hand and he slashed me repeatedly across my shoulder, and I started to bleed, the blood gushing down my arm. After a bit, when the blood slowed somewhat, he raised the razor again and cut the fleshy part of my arm. More gushing blood, and when that slowed he slashed me on my side, and I saw that he intended to kill me as the razor slashed again and again … I screamed. Out loud. Which woke me. I sat up in bed, heart thumping. The clock under the ever-burning light said five minutes after two. A guard came running in response to my screams. I explained I had been dreaming a slasher dream about the judge.

"That's a common enough dream in here," she answered. "Judges occupy a heavy place in inmates' dreams. Just try not to scream, okay? It upsets the other women."

Okay. Only I couldn't really get back to sleep. But I am now very anxious to get to court. None of the other inmates are up yet, so I try to be quiet. I eat a bite of toast and take only a sip of the coffee. I love coffee, but not when I'm in a tense situation. Tense situations make me want to pee and coffee compounds the urge. And I know very well that this entire day will be tense.

After trying to make myself halfway presentable for court, I am let out of my unit. With my legal papers in hand, I make my way down to the records and receiving departments. Half a dozen other women are going to court this morning, too. We are all searched and put into a holding cell. We could be in this cell for an hour, so one might as well lie back and not sweat the small stuff. One woman was recently picked up from the street and is still dope sick. There's usually at least one in this condition in any given court haul, sometimes more. The sick one is stretched out on the long bench, which doesn't leave a lot of room for the rest of us, but nobody asks the sick woman to sit up. We make do in silent sympathy. Most of these women have been in the same ghastly space where this woman is, just trying to survive. Except for the plump older Asian woman. She doesn't use, she sells. In quantity. Maybe she won't anymore. She is facing the possibility of heavy time.

Some of the women know me, or know about me. They are curious about why I do what I do. But only mildly. Their own lives are so scrambled, their worries so immediate, they haven't much room for speculation outside their physical needs. But I consider them political prisoners, too. If all the women at BCCW who had been arrested for drug or drug-related offences were released, I would be the only one left in my unit and one of the few left in the entire prison. It is all just too incredibly stupid to be borne.

At 7:20 a.m. the sheriffs finally arrive. This is the fun part. We are searched again by the sheriffs and then we go into another waiting unit. There we kneel on the long bench against the wall and a sheriff puts on the leg irons and then the handcuffs. The sheriffs on the whole are relatively pleasant and will ease the clasp of the leg irons or handcuffs a bit if one complains loudly. And something has changed since my outburst in court over the shoelaces. Now I'm allowed to keep them in my shoes. And the sheriffs, both women and men, have always been nice about lending me a hand to get into and out of the police van. I'll just let these nice sheriffs help me, even though I could probably take at least a couple down in a street fight. But the seats in the sheriff's wagon are straight from hell. The benches are metal and the windows are only open a crack.

It's still early morning but the air is warm, close, swampy. There isn't any breeze. When the wagon turns a corner sharply or stops abruptly we all slide together up and down the bench, crunching together in the most intimate way until we can straighten ourselves under the burden of handcuffs and leg irons. A couple of the women yell to the officers in front to turn up the radio full blast. The officers comply. My favourite station, too: Rock 101. The loud, raucous music pounds at my head as we ride through the streets of Vancouver. We can see out the side windows of the van. I can look at the people driving to work in their cars but they can't see me. The sick woman moans and curses, coughs and gags. I try to position my feet to miss the splash in case she vomits. But no, she's holding firm in spite of the threatening noises. We stop on the way to pick up two male prisoners. When the men get in, several of the young women perk up and initiate conversation through the partition that allows occupants to see each other.

The flirtations seem so normal somehow, in spite of the crude language. There are inquiries about legal status, what one is in for, how long, is one going for probation, reduced charges, electronic monitoring? And then the older of the two male prisoners notices me.

"Hey, what's a lady doing in here?" he asks loudly, staring at me. "What in the hell did you do?"

"Oh, it was just a robbery that went bad," I say impulsively.

His eyes pop. "No shit!"

The women laugh.

"She's a tree hugger," Blue Bell explains. Blue Bell is a Native woman. She is young and tall and healthy looking. She uses crack, but she doesn't inject. She smokes it. She's already been in jail a year, so she has recovered from the physical deterioration caused by her addiction. But that addiction led her into serious crime. Her offence really was a robbery that went bad. She's going to court to testify in another case.

"A tree hugger! What's that?"

Blue Bell explains why I was arrested.

"You're in jail just for standing in the middle of a logging road? Holy shit!"

"That's fucking crazy, man," the other, older male prisoner says quietly. "Locking up a nice old lady for trying to save a tree."

"Well, it wasn't just a tree," I begin.

"No. Fuck, man, it was a whole forest of trees," Blue Bell goes on. "In a place called the Elaho. It's out there by Squamish. They have thousand-year-old trees there. And grizzly bears and stuff. A real forest."

I look at Blue Bell in astonishment. She has never given the slightest indication of being remotely interested in anything I have said about the forests—or anything else, for that matter.

"A real forest?" the older one asks. "Shit, that's something. Where is this fucking Elaho? Maybe I'll go out there if I ever get out of the fucking joint. Excuse my language, lady. You know what I mean."

"Yes, of course," I say. And I tell him how to get out to the Elaho. I've told several different people in the sheriff's vans how to get to the Elaho. If any of them actually go, wouldn't that be something? Wouldn't that just fix it with this judge, who seems convinced that we anti-logging protesters are all criminals anyway? The very idea makes me laugh. But by the time I am actually escorted into the courtroom, my funny bone has withered. I can tell right off it's going to be a helluva day.

David Haffey is present to testify. Robbie Fleming, a bright young defence lawyer who is representing Reasha Wolfe, who was also charged for blockading logging trucks in the Elaho, asks Mr. Justice Parrett to excuse himself as judge of the proceedings on the grounds of bias. I ask, from the prisoner's box, for a stay of proceedings on he grounds that because I was arrested under an injunction instead of the Criminal Code, as are all other Canadians under like circumstances, I was denied my rights under the Charter. Both applications are refused "tout court." Mr. Haffey is called to the witness stand. The show goes on.

Under cross-examination, Mr. Haffey tries to explain what happened on September 15, 1999, at the protest camp in the Elaho Valley. He is sticking to his second explanation, which was that he had taken the videotape of the attack on the camp and thrown it over the Lava Creek bridge. He insists that nobody told him to do it, he did it of his own volition.

The trouble with this story is that after Mr. Haffey's first testimony, Derek Sayle, who is Mr. Haffey's superior, gave a different explanation. Mr. Sayle was also present in the Elaho on the day of the attack, and he told the court that he had ordered Mr. Haffey to toss the tape over the bridge. Why did Mr. Sayle tell such a different story? It just doesn't make sense. Of course, Mr. Haffey is trying to protect his higher-ups, but Mr. Sayle's testimony is truly puzzling. And another peculiar thing I have heard—because even in prison one hears things—is that Hugh Sutcliffe, one of the vice presidents of Interfor, was also in the Elaho on the day of the attack. If true, this might explain something. But what? I am getting a headache.

I should have stayed out of the courtroom after I walked out the first time, instead of playing these courtroom games. Shortly before I walked out I had dismissed Robert Moore-Stewart as my attorney. I felt that we accused were being dispensed with like so much legal garbage, and our case was not being reported in the daily newspapers or on TV. I had to do something to bring what I considered Interfor's forest crimes to public attention. So I dismissed Robert, much to Mr. Justice Parrett's alarm, and told the court I considered the trial an absolute sham and would no longer honour it with my presence. Mr. Justice Parrett said I would be arrested if I tried to leave the courtroom. I was not a prisoner at that time, as I had been released on a promise to keep the peace, but as I was representing myself, I had to be in the courtroom during the trial. Mr. Justice Parrett was as good as his word. I tried to leave and was arrested and taken upstairs to be booked into the courthouse cells before being sent back to Burnaby.

The matron in charge of the women's cells, who was by this time more than a nodding acquaintance, was right cross with me. "What are you doing up here?" she demanded as a deputy sheriff undid my handcuffs. "You're supposed to be downstairs in the courtroom."

"I'm mad at the judge," I answered, emptying the contents of my handbag onto her desk as ordered.

"That's no good reason," she said, shuffling through my belongings. "Everybody that's up here in these cells is mad at some judge or other. You can't just come up here every time you get mad at the judge." She paused, looking at a petrified kidney bean that a friend had given me. It was polished smooth, like an ancient stone. "What's this?" she asked suspiciously, holding the bean up to the light.

"It's a lucky bean," I answered.

I watched her write down on the prisoner's incoming item sheet: one bean, lucky. That struck me as being hilariously funny. I laughed until the tears ran down my cheeks. I was probably hysterical.

The upshot of that day was that the judge made a decision that I didn't have to be in the courtroom, and he ordered my release. I had advised him that if he tried to force me to remain in the courtroom I would have to be bound and gagged; perhaps this swayed his decision.

That evening I got together with a few friends and made signs declaring that Interfor had hijacked the court. The next morning we picketed the Supreme Court building. It was at this point that Mr. Justice Parrett recessed our case until Mr. Haffey could return to testify. And I'm sure he was pleased that the recess would also interrupt my picketing.

I still think the whole trial is a farce and a waste of taxpayers' money, but I've been participating in the game.

Back in my unit at BCWW I make my way to the phones while the others go out for track, which means most go outside to smoke and gossip. I call Sue, the eldest of my daughters, first. I chat with her in Pennsylvania, then with Margaret Elizabeth and Rose Mary in Ucluelet, and after, I try to call my three boys one by one. Of course my boys are almost as old as I am now, but they're still my boys and must be brought up to date. They can't call me in the prison, so I have to call them.

Joey, my eldest, lives and works in California. He has a terrific job in the electronics business, but he is, at the moment, quite troubled. The terrific job doesn't satisfy him; he is an artist. He sculpts in bronze and paints in oils. He's in the midst of a midlife crisis. He loves two different women, tries to satisfy both, makes both miserable, as well as himself. At times he would like to chuck everything and become a penniless artist before both women get fed up and chuck him. I can't help. What do I know of sexual and romantic relationships, what does anybody know? Each couple might as well be Adam and Eve, or Adam and Lilith, or in this case, Adam and Eve and Lilith. Whatever. Next I call the answering service of my middle son, Mike.

Mike will not be in. He is always out in the bush somewhere; at the moment he's in northern Manitoba. He will be sketching the scenery, prospecting for gold, discovering and naming new rivers and creeks after himself and friends and relatives, trying out the snowshoes, Damascus knives or birchbark canoe that he has painstakingly made for his adventures. He will carve and write poetry and short stories, far from the reaches of civilization.

Mike is out of touch for months on end, but I've stopped worrying. The man has an arts degree and a reputation as a sculptor. If he could tolerate cities he could command serious money for his work. But he can't. He has the wilderness gene in spades. I pity him. He inherited it from me. Had I just stayed out of the bush and refrained from hobnobbing with the trees and creeks and streams and bears and cougars and smaller, less threatening forest critters, I wouldn't be in prison now, with more time to come. After I leave a message with the answering service, which isn't likely to hear from Mike any time soon, I call my third son, Andy.

I'm concerned about Andy's health. Andy is a musician. Musicians aren't known to think of health unless it can somehow be put to music. After Andy's scare with cancer he seemed to be earnest about changing his stress levels. But his whole life has revolved around music, and even though he now produces for other artists more than he performs himself, the music business is synonymous with stress. I find Andy at home in Toronto, ready to report. Is he eating vegetables, taking vitamins, not smoking? He assures me all is well with him and his family unit. Satisfied, I give up the phone and turn my attention to my own unit. There seems to be some sort of commotion going on.

Two new inmates have arrived. The discussion about what rooms they will be stuffed into becomes lively. Just not mine, I pray silently to the Mother of us all. Since Suzanne was released, I have had the cell to myself. This is extremely important to me. Not because I don't want to share other women's misery, but because I don't want to share desk space. This is the only area where I ever deliberately pulled rank on Suzanne. Because I monopolized the desk, she more often than not had to take her own writing out into the common room, where bedlam reigns.

But I am relatively safe from double-bunking because I don't smoke. Everybody else does. Smoking is no longer allowed in the common rooms, so women must smoke in their cells, except during assigned track times. Smokers can't be bunked in with non-smokers, although I get smoke nevertheless. It seeps out of half-opened doors, clings to inmates' clothes and breath, blows in the wind outside in the exercise yard.

I have to concentrate: tomorrow I will cross-examine David Haffey.

The problem is, I feel sorry for Mr. Haffey in one and the same breath that I resent him taking up so much of our court time. He isn't a bad person, and he doesn't look well. He is a worried, rather sick man. And I understand some of his worries. When he says he threw the tape into the river because he was fearful of what the tape's disclosure might bring, I sympathize. Fear of ostracism, loss of job, loss of status, loss of home.

I've been in that place, that agony, during the school integration struggles in the deep South. I lived out this dilemma in the early Vietnam War protests, felt its sting when I protested patriarchy in its most entrenched, dreadful forms. What I yearn to tell Mr. Haffey is go where your humanity leads you, man, it has led you this far. You are the only one connected with Interfor who has recognized that something occurred that infamous day in the woods in the Elaho that shouldn't have, that your friends and co-workers acted in a shameful manner, that your bosses acted in an unfeeling, inglorious way. In recognizing this you have a choice: you can either go forward with your insights or you can refuse. You can walk through the swamp of moral struggle, which is populated with alligators and poisonous snakes and swamp spiders as big as your fist, until you come out the other side; and while there is no guarantee that you will come out the other side, if you do, you will not be afraid anymore and that is the most liberating thrill known to man or woman. It makes you free, man, it makes you free. Your children will regard you with awe even as they may decry their loss of pretty things; your wife will complain and worry about the future, but she may also (perhaps secretly) regard you as more of a man; your friends and co-workers will turn their backs on you, but they will be impressed, nevertheless, and you will make them wonder ...

But of course I don't say any of these things when it is my turn to cross-examine Mr. Haffey the next day. Mr. Haffey is not ready for walks through the swamp. He's just trying to survive. I ask a few questions. "What did you think, Mr. Haffey, when you heard that your boss, Mr. Sayle, had come forward on the stand with the information that he, Mr. Sayle, had ordered you, Mr. Haffey, to throw the tape over the bridge?" Mr. Haffey replies that he thought Mr. Sayle had gone crazy, because it wasn't true, he had done the deed all by himself. I ask if he knew that Mr. Hugh Sutcliffe, vice president of Interfor, was in the Elaho the day of the attack for a meeting at noon with Mr. David Miller, operations manager, just as the forest workers of Interfor and their contractors were amassing to attack the protest camp? No, he didn't know that. I thank him, wish him luck, and thus conclude my cross-examination. Rick McCallion, a self-represented person, asks some further questions, but nothing more of substance is to be had from Mr. Haffey's testimony.

Before court is over for the day, I mention that I have subpoenaed Andrew Petter, the Attorney General of British Columbia, to appear at ten o'clock the next morning. The judge smiles. It's one of those unsmiley smiles. I don't like it. He can smile nicely; I've seen him do it a couple of times. When he does a real smile, it changes his entire demeanour, it makes him look friendly, flexible, reasonable, a man with a rather quirky sense of humour, a man who can swing with the punches. And he can even laugh. I heard him do it—not once, but twice. But that event is not likely to repeat itself now.

When I get back to BCWW I have enough tofu waiting for me to soothe my troubled soul. Very few of the other inmates will eat tofu. Evidently it was on the evening's menu, as there are a dozen untouched servings in the refrigerator. "It's all for you, Betty," a couple of the women exclaim generously. I taste it. Sweet and sour style. Not bad. It's certainly an improvement over the frozen dinners saved for women who have to be in court and come back too late for the dinner trays. But my enjoyment of the tofu is ruined by the conversation of the two young women sitting at the next table playing cards.

"No, don't worry, the guys around here like big girls," Evening Fire is saying to one of the new inmates in a low, confidential tone. Ordinarily I would not be able to hear conversation from an adjoining table in the common room because of the continuous high-volume babble of gossip, information sharing and misinformation sharing, punctuated with equal measures of raucous laughter and angry accusations, but at the moment there is some sort of exciting movie on in the TV room. The women at the table next to me are the only other occupants of the common area and they are so intent on their conversation they are oblivious to my presence. Usually the women are somewhat careful what they say around me, not so much from distrust as simply a lack of an appropriate category in which to place me. I get a kind of guarded respect and a rather wide berth, but it isn't wide enough at the moment.

Night Breeze, the new inmate, is tall and big-boned, and she seems to be somewhat worried about her size.

"Hell, yes, you'll make a pile of it," Evening Fire goes on. "I know the best fucking places on the east side to work," she continues, not realizing her double entendre. Or maybe she does. Maybe it's an old joke. "I'm out of here in a few weeks. I can set you up if you're into it."

Evening Fire has gained thirty pounds in the six weeks she's been incarcerated. She weighed ninety-seven pounds when she came in. She had been on an up streak, using every day, not eating, just using, hooking, using again, until after days, weeks, her self-protective senses mostly gone, she took too much—"chickened," as they call it, right downtown. Ambulance, brief medical attention, arrest for possession or possession with intent to traffic, off to jail, back to BCWW, downtime in segregation, released back into the general prison population when she could keep food down and stop shaking. She will be released back to the east side of Vancouver very shortly. Multiply her story by the hundreds, by the thousands, even, with only a few variations: Instead of overdosing, selling drugs or sex to undercover officers, or robbing a john, or stealing credit cards, clothes, anything loose—and they will be back in BCWW. This is what the Burnaby Correctional Centre for Women is mostly about. Drugs and petty crime.

Recidivism. A fancy-sounding word for repeated incarcerations. But then, of course, I'm a recidivist myself. This is my fourth sojourn in this joint. And I have lots of work to do tonight. I have to think about just exactly what I will ask the Attorney General should he actually show up in the morning. But I can't think. My mind is stuck on my sister inmates' conversation.

I turn in early, unable to think, and stare at the ceiling. I try to conjure up my notion of the Goddess, of ancestresses, but the familiar composite of female deities and deceased female heroes doesn't materialize. What does materialize is my mother's face and our conversation following Aunt Gladys' meeting with the aliens. I find myself relaxing, remembering, smiling into the soft glare of the prison's gaze ...

Chapter Four

After Mama got Aunt Gladys settled in with the aliens at the hospital in Mississippi over the phone, she wanted some iced tea.

"It's so late, Mama," I said, glancing at the clock. Twelve-thirty. But it was still hot enough to fry a slice of hog fat on the hoof. "Won't it keep you from sleeping?"

"Aw, iced tea never kept anybody from sleeping. You kids used to drink barrels of it when you were little and you slept just fine."

Maybe, I thought, as I filled up two tall glasses with ice cubes. It's true we drank barrels of iced tea as kids. But I can remember having lots of nightmares. Was the tea responsible, or do all kids have nightmares? My own kids had their share, at least the girls did. In fact, they felt compelled to complain to me every time one of them had a nightmare, as though I could have prevented it from occurring: I was the mother, wasn't I? Why wasn't I on the job as nightmare deflector?

I followed Mama out to the front porch with the iced tea. It was a wonderful night. Except for the heat, which crept out from underneath the house and enveloped the porch like a steam blanket. But the insect party had reached a peak. Oh, what dancing and singing and merrymaking! The myriad insects were reeling with their own power of communication with the universe. They are the true children of the earth, they are the majority of all creatures, they were here before and will be here after, they are indispensable, indestructible. They are the power and they are rocking …

"I don't sit out much at night with Gladys anymore," Mama said, propping her feet up on a cushion. "The mosquitoes eat her up."

"It's because she didn't have malaria," I venture. "I read where mosquitoes won't bite people who have had malaria."

"I read that, too. I almost died from malaria when I was young. But you never had malaria and mosquitoes don't bite you, either."

"Maybe it was some antibody you passed on to me in mother's milk."

"I don't remember if I even nursed you. If I did it wasn't for very long."

This was shocking news. I had always thought of myself as having been lovingly breast-fed as a baby.

"I nursed Doris because she was so puny and the doctor thought she might not survive," Mama continued.

Oh, fine. Doris was breast-fed but I got the bottle. I felt a prick of almost forgotten sibling rivalry. Doris had been dead twenty years, but as a kid I resented the special treats Mama would make for her. She often had to be coaxed to eat. And now I learn that Doris got the biggest treat of all, and I didn't. Well.

Breast-fed or not, Doris certainly took to the bottle after she grew up, and it was the bottle that eventually took her away to permanent dreamland. That and pills. I loved my sister, but our relationship was strained. She played a very hard game of "See what you made me do" from the time of my earliest memory. As a child, if crossed, she would hold her breath until she turned blue and passed out. As an adult she substituted pills and liquor for the breath-holding. Her family learned early to tiptoe around her. She held us all hostage, but after she died an early death I sorely missed her.

I missed just knowing my sister was in her place, in her nice little

house in Baton Rouge, busy trying to balance her outer world of being a nurse, studying for a degree and managing kids, husband and
home, with her inner world of disappointments, dissatisfactions and
addictions. I didn't know how to help her. She always made me feel
that I was the one who needed help. And as I was a lot less stable in
marriage and place of residence than she was, there was always a large
amount of truth in her sisterly observations. And so I would give way
in our infrequent discussions about the seriousness of her drinking
and prescription drug habits. But in hindsight, I shouldn't have.

At my sister's funeral the church overflowed with flowers and
mourners—relatives, yes, but also many strangers who wept at my
sister's passing, people whose lives she had touched in her capacity as
a palliative care nurse ...

"Mama, do you still miss Doris?" I asked abruptly.

"Do you still miss Barbara?" Mama countered gently.

"But it's only been two and a half years for me," I protest. "Does it
ever go away?"

"No. Never. You can't hope for that. But after a while you don't
want it to go away. She was part of you, the missing her will become
part of you, too. Right now I just hope Gladys rallies. She's not ready
to go. She's afraid."

"So how come you're not afraid?" I asked softly, and then wanted
to bite my tongue. I already knew the answer. Mama was religious in
the traditional sense.

"Because it's just something else that has to be reckoned with,"
she answered evenly. "It's there, so you just do it."

I laughed. So it wasn't religion that made her unafraid of death,
just a very practical turn of mind that considered death simply
another obligation, a duty, if you will.

She peered at me over the top of her glass. The light from the living room cast a diffused shadow across the porch, wrapping our private space into that of the night.

"What's so funny?" she asked suspiciously.

"You're funny."

"I'm glad I'm amusing you."

I tinkled the ice in my glass and then pressed the glass to my damp forehead. Out from under the air conditioners one became impressed with one's mortality. And maybe, just maybe, we had both already died and this was hell.

"Well, tell me a story," I demanded. "As long as we're up. Tell me about the olden days."

"No, Betty."

"Yes, Mama."

Mama loved stories. I think that's why she married Daddy. He kept her entertained with stories. When the going got tough, the tough got funnier. Mama's humour was droller than Daddy's. Her stories were not as wide ranging, but I thought her funnier. She sipped at her iced tea for a moment, searching for a story.

"Well, let me see. Did I ever tell you about the nurse who came around when we lived in Gum Carbo?"

"No, Mama. That's one I haven't heard."

"Poppa was running a sawmill and we lived so far out in the piney woods this public health nurse had to hire a local man to direct her to where she could find some kids. She was doing a report on what types of intestinal parasites young 'uns had in that neck of the woods.

"The nurse wanted us each to smear a little tad of our bowel movements on these little glass slides that she left, and label which was which. Mama wasn't feeling well and didn't feel up to the task, so because I was the eldest, she turned the whole business over to me. The nurse said she would be back the day after, so I promptly tended to my glass slide and your Aunt Sit turned in hers to me without any problem, but your Aunt Gladys became troubled by the entire exercise. Some kind of performance anxiety, I guess. She got constipated. She was only six years old, so I went with her to the outhouse several times and she'd sit and strain but she couldn't do anything."

Mama paused, sipping at her tea again.

"So what happened?" I asked, unable to see where this story was going.

"Well, the morning the nurse was supposed to come back, Gladys had a panic attack. She cried and cried because she couldn't do anything and she mightily didn't want to disappoint the nurse. So Gladys asked me for her glass slide and said maybe she could do something by herself without me standing around waiting. So I gave her the slide and she went out back with it. And it wasn't long before she came looking for me with a brown stain caught neatly between the slender sections of glass. I washed the sides of the slide and Gladys' hands thoroughly with hot soap and water the way the nurse had instructed, and when she arrived I delivered all three samples proudly into her hands. We had all done our part as concerned citizens of Mississippi.

"After the nurse left I told Gladys to take off her shoes. The shoes were just for the nurse's benefit and had to be cleaned up good for Sunday. But when I picked up the shoes where Gladys had left them on the back porch, I noticed the brown speckled stains on the sides of both shoes. I grabbed Gladys just as she was shimmying up the treehouse tree out by the driveway.

"'You've been in the chicken yard,' I yelled at her. She wasn't supposed to go in the chicken yard alone because of an ole bad rooster we had. He jumped Gladys once and scratched her arm and Gladys had a fit and it upset Mama. Mama was seriously ill by then and we were all supposed to stay out of trouble.

"Gladys pulled away from me and started bawling. Which surprised me. 'Why are you blubbering?' I asked her. 'I just want you to stay out of the chicken yard. Why were you in there, anyway?' 'I had to go in there,' she sobbed. 'Why?' I demanded. 'To get some chicken shit …' " Mama's voice trailed off, chuckling.

"And then I knew what the nurse had hauled away in Gladys' sample, all neatly labelled," Mama added.

I laughed. "So what happened? Did the nurse ever find out?"

"Not that I know of. That's the peculiar part. Either us kids and the chickens had the same parasites and they weren't harmful, or else all of us, including the chickens, were clean of whatever they were looking for."

"But surely whoever was doing the testing must have noticed that one of the samples was chicken shit."

"Well, I wouldn't put money on it. The nurse mentioned that the samples were going to somewhere up north for testing. New York, I think Poppa said, and he wasn't surprised we never heard back because those northern people probably never saw a chicken before, and how could they possibly know what chicken shit looked like?"

"Mama, that tops the drunk chicken story," I said. "But tell about the drunk chickens again, while we're on the subject."

"Oh, you've heard that story a million times," Mama replied.

"I know, but I love it," I wheedled. And I did, too. The drunk chicken story was about when Mama and Daddy were first married, during Prohibition, years before Daddy got religion, and they were making bootleg corn whiskey. A chicken and egg farm masked the illegal operation. One day Daddy unthinkingly threw the leftover corn mash from the whiskey-making process out to the chickens. Leftover mash has a high alcohol content, and the chickens got roaring drunk the very afternoon the Prohibition officers, acting on a tip, stopped by my parents' chicken farm.

Daddy feigned innocence all through the drunken performance the chickens played out before the two astonished officers. The roosters were trying to fight each other but were too drunk to connect, and the hens were dragging their wings in the dirt as they went around in circles. One rooster made a run for one of the hens, missed, and ran head first into the wooden fence, falling senseless right at the officers' feet. One of the officers laughed out loud but the other one said he'd be back with a search warrant. Mama and Daddy got rid of the chickens and the still and that ended their flirtation with living outside the law. It was hard times, Mama would explain when this brief period of their lives came up in conversation.

Now Mama drained the last of the iced tea from her glass. "Ask me tomorrow," she said. "I think I'm ready for bed now. I feel sleepy."

And I do, too. The memory of Mama's voice and the stories of the public health nurse and the chickens have wiped the events of the day in court out of my head. I am being lulled to sleep despite the glare of the prison light and the sounds of lockdown as the prison guard starts on the bottom tier, each door shutting with a clang. I can count the clangs as the guard moves from door to door. She's upstairs now, one, two, three, at my own door, the grating clang as it closes, the firm click of the huge key she carries on her key ring. I am locked behind a steel door, locked up, locked down, locked ...

But I have conquered my fear of being locked in small spaces. I faced this down in the struggles over Clayoquot Sound. After four and a half months of incarceration then, and months of Elaho-inspired incarceration now—much of which has been spent in city jail cells or courtroom cells—I could probably step into a steel-sided cracker box and not feel inconvenienced. I sleep well, and when I wake I'm refreshed, ready for another round of the courtroom game.

Today I will know if the Attorney General will respond to my subpoena. I have also subpoenaed another gentleman, Jeffery Gall, from the Attorney General's office. I have subpoenaed him because when I cross-examined Sergeant Brian, the arresting officer in the Elaho RCMP detachment, he said that a Mr. Jeffery Gall had explained the procedure to him for arresting anti-logging protesters. I want to know why it is that anti-logging protesters are treated in a special way. Why are we are not arrested for infractions of the law that we commit, like blocking a public road? Instead we are arrested under an injunction that results in charges of contempt of court. The RCMP wouldn't wait around for an injunction before making an arrest if a drunk person pitched a tent in the middle of a public road.

I am deeply angry about court-ordered injunctions against environmental activists. They are undemocratic. They strip me and all protesters of our rights under the Charter of Rights and Freedoms. I want to be treated like a common criminal. I insist upon it. When I break a law, it is my right to be treated like all other lawbreakers in British Columbia. Mr. Petter, the Attorney General, has introduced a discussion paper in Parliament on the possibility of legislation to circumvent the SLAPP suits that logging companies initiate, which give rise to the injunctions that result in charges of contempt of court. SLAPP stands for Strategic Lawsuits Against Public Participation. Its very name is telling: The lawsuits are designed to threaten citizens who feel compelled to indulge in public participation. What it means is that defenders of public property can be sued privately and may face the loss of their property and money, if they have any. SLAPP lawsuits deprive citizens of basic human, oral and civil rights. And perhaps Mr. Petter can tell the court, tell me, tell all of us, how he came to the conclusion that SLAPP suits are not in the best interests of citizens and why it is, then, that I am standing before this court on a charge that he believes is bogus and prejudicial. Mr. Petter should welcome the opportunity to step forward and put some sense into these proceedings.

But no, Mr. Andrew Petter isn't any more ready for gutsy confrontation of the issues than David Haffey was. And maybe Mr. Petter doesn't like me because I organized a picket in front of his office in Vancouver and sent numerous applications to him to intervene in this trial with a stay of proceedings. But at least Mr. Petter sent a nice lawyer to explain why he had sent the nice lawyer in his place.

It isn't very convincing. Mr. Groberman argues that Mr. Petter shouldn't be made to come to court because of something in common law dating back to the fourteenth century. Something about attorney generals having immunity from being summoned to court when Parliament was in session, and if a judge had the audacity to summon an attorney general (were they even called attorney generals in those days?), the judge could be sentenced to three days in the tower. Or some such nonsense. Ridiculous.

I get up and say so, reiterating that the Attorney General should want to come to this court to straighten out some of these pressing issues. He's the Attorney General, isn't he? This is a far-reaching question, isn't it? It concerns everyone in British Columbia because it concerns our public property. But no, Mr. Justice Parrett rules that neither the Attorney General nor his colleague need come to court because of political reasons, among other things. Political reasons? Are we not all political? I'm trying to defend myself in court. How is that more political than the decision to place anti-logging protesters in a special arrest-and-charge category? I swear, they all remind me of the churches back in Louisiana during the crisis of school integration. The very agencies who have some clout to remedy a situation decline to get involved.

There is a courtroom break right after the judge's ruling. Upon our return Mr. Justice Parrett looks at me and smiles. A real smile.

"Anyway," he says, "I'm sure Mrs. Krawczyk wouldn't want to see me locked up in the tower for three days."

Oh, wouldn't I? I think he is somewhat worried that after his ruling, I might pick up my marbles and refuse to play anymore. Earlier in the trial, when I left his courtroom before the adjournment and went outside and picketed the proceedings in front of the courthouse steps, he was not happy. So now he's making a joke.

"I would rethink that, sir," I answer lightly. And I don't walk out, because Mr. Flanz has wrapped up the Crown's case and it is now our turn to start the defence. But there is an embarrassing pause in the proceedings. Nobody seems ready to begin the defence. I look to Les Mackoff, counsel for Camille Willicome. Les is friendly and capable and should be the first one up for the defence. But no, he says he isn't quite ready with his witnesses.

The ball goes next to Robbie Fleming. Robbie is counsel for Reasha Wolfe and Chris Nolan. Robbie is young and charming, easily the judge's favourite defence lawyer, if the judge could be said to have one. But Robbie needs time to polish his defence, too. Richard Brooks is next, staunch defender of Dennis Porter. He, too, passes.

He needs more time. Don Gardner, counsel for Justin Paine and Chris Keats, follows Richard Brooks in line of order. Don is big, imposing. But he needs more time, too, for his clients.

That leaves me next in line, followed by Rick McCallion and then Barney Kern. Barney has discharged his attorney and is now representing himself. That makes three of us who are self-represented. But neither Rick nor Barney is quite ready, either. Yet something has to happen here. Things can't just be left dangling. My Southern country upbringing rises to the fore.

I don't know what it is with Southern women. We're not overly taught the rules needed to grease the wheels of Southern country society, but we absorb them by osmosis. We learn at a gut level that it's our fault if social interactions bog down, that it's our duty to prevent this, that others' social comfort is a woman's responsibility—be it at a house party, a church social or a meeting of field hands. People must be put at their ease, particularly menfolk; if they aren't engaged with each other in a friendly way they might start bristling at each other. No Southern woman will allow an awkward lull in a conversation to become long, and all guests must be honoured, particularly the guest of honour, which in this instance must be the judge, since we are all facing him, paying homage, waiting on his pleasure, so to speak. He must not be inconvenienced by a perceived lack of progress in the courtroom, so I offer myself up as the sacrificial lamb. I will be the first to open the defence in the morning, and I will be my own first witness.

I will have to work late when I get back to BCWW, maybe far into the night. I feel in my heart that Mr. Justice Parrett is prejudiced against us as a group, although he seems to make an exception of me in some instances, occasionally exhibiting a kind of grudging respect.

He even said he had read my book, *Clayoquot: The Sound of my Heart*, when I offered to give him a copy. Of course, he might have said that just to be nice, or to save me from actually giving him a copy. Anyway, while Mr. Justice Parrett gets angry at me from time to time, he treats me rather gently at other times. I am, after all, an elder. But I agree with Suzanne Jackson that he probably wishes we could all be sent to a military boot camp for an extended period. His mind just cannot get around the fact that he wrote an order and we disobeyed it. Nothing else matters to him.

When I get on the witness stand in the morning, I want to try to talk to him in a human way. I want to try to explain honestly how I came to be in the space I occupied, what led me to it, what forces propelled me, a seventy-one-year-old woman, to go out to an isolated logging road and try to stop Interfor logging trucks. I will take my time and try to persuade him to see what I see, to feel what I feel, to walk in my shadow for a brief time.

When I get back to my cell at BCWW that evening I am in for a rude shock. A strange stack of clothes is sitting in one corner of my cell and a bunch of equally strange books and papers have been thrown across my desk. The extra mattress that had been neatly stored underneath my bunk after Suzanne's departure has been dragged out and arranged in the middle of the floor. I have been assigned a cellmate. Bloody hell!

Chapter Five

Tonight I desperately need my desk space, and I must have some quiet time to arrange my thoughts for court tomorrow. Surely there has been a mistake that I should acquire a roommate just at this crucial time in my life. I make a beeline for the unit office.

"And I don't smoke," I add to the list of reasons why I can't double-bunk at this time.

"She doesn't smoke, either," the guard says, looking up at me from behind her desk. A nice woman, actually. East Indian. Beautiful dark eyes and a calm, unhurried manner. "And she's American."

"I don't care," I say, my voice rising in frustration. "Anyway, I'm Canadian now. And I need my space. I represent myself in court and tomorrow I have to put myself on the witness stand and I have to know what questions I will be asking myself ... don't you see?"

"Betty, I'm sorry. She has been sent here and she must be put somewhere. You are the only other non-smoker on the unit so I have to put her in with you."

Oh, I want to rant and rave and stomp my foot and show the women in here that Granny knows a few choice cuss words herself. But I don't. These people have their rules. They are not the enemy. I keep a very clear image in my head of exactly who the enemy is, and I don't like to get sidetracked. I retreat to my room to organize myself as best as I can. It occurs to me that I could ask to go to segregation. It would be quieter there and I could think. But going to segregation voluntarily probably won't be allowed, and even if it were, I don't think inmates are allowed to take pens and papers and books and legal documents. Best just to tough it out here in the unit, I decide. With the mattress in the middle of the floor there is no point in worrying about desk space because I won't be able to get to the desk anyway. So I just heave all of my working papers onto my bunk. And my new roommate, having complied with all the checking-in at the desk that this particular hotel requires, steps into what is now our joint abode.

She seems pleasant enough. She is, or has been, a legal secretary. She was arrested for taking her little boy out of a group home in California and crossing the border with him. He had been taken away from her because of alleged abuse by her boyfriend. She seems intelligent and articulate, and she denies abuse on anyone's part. I listen. I explain to her that she doesn't have to explain anything to me, but she seems to want to. At least she isn't dope sick. Not being dope sick has become my criterion for acceptable conduct. Just about anything else can be excused.

My new roommate graciously withdraws to her mattress while I spread out my papers on top of my bunk. I don't stop writing until the large light is turned off at a main switch and the smaller light grows too dim for my scribbling. Then I give up and put my things away underneath my bunk. I'm tired, but restless. And I'm hungry. I barely touched the frozen dinner. But it is too late to eat anything now. My stomach rumbles, precluding sleep. I think about each of my children, touching them with my concern. And Barbara. Barbara Ellen. She is on a journey I can't know. Not yet. It was Mama who helped me through that dreadful time, who told me what to expect when the shadows closed in. I can hear someone sobbing in the next cell. I hate that more than anything, to hear these women, caged here like animals, sobbing in the night. Mama, tell me a story, tell me something funny ...

•

"Oh, Betty, you get something in your head you just can't let it go," Mama said after we had come back from visiting Aunt Gladys in the hospital. It was the day after the alien episode. Aunt Gladys had her senses back and was embarrassed about the aliens. I wasn't going to elaborate on her conversation with them (simply out of politeness), but she said the dumplings were scorched and spat them out into her napkin and after that I figured it was okay to talk about the aliens since she had already stepped over the line. I was on a roll until Mama told me to hush. The doctor said Aunt Gladys could come home the next day and I found that depressing, so when Mama suggested we stop by Kentucky Fried Chicken for lunch on the way home, I said okay. We bought a small family pack take-out order.

I'm a vegetarian. At home, I am. With Mama and Aunt Gladys I give it up. They are such extraordinary cooks that the meat they serve up doesn't taste like meat, anyway, it tastes like heaven. Besides, they don't use a lot of meat. Meat is for seasoning, meat is to complement rice and peppers and garlic and onions, turnip greens and dumplings. One only eats hunks of meat on occasion. Kentucky Fried Chicken is one such occasion.

Kentucky Fried Chicken tastes different down South than it does in Canada. It's crisper, spicier, and luscious biscuits are served with even the smallest order. The Colonel's Mississippi biscuits are crisp and butter-browned on the outside, tender and flaky on the inside.

Almost as good as Mama's. Canadians don't understand biscuits, or even the necessity for them. I've never eaten a Canadian biscuit. If you ask for a biscuit in a Canadian restaurant the server will bring you a cookie. To have biscuits at home I have to make them myself, and making biscuits has never been my strong point. When I mentioned how good the biscuits smelled as I took them gently out of the box, Mama said it wasn't long ago that a woman's biscuits, not her looks, got her a good husband. I wasn't sure I believed that. After all, I'd had four husbands and they never tasted my biscuits until after marriage, any more than they did my intimate embrace, so to speak. But that's what Mama said. I figured it was a small point so I let her have it. Anyway, one could argue that my first two husbands weren't exactly good. But we have spread our feast out on the kitchen table with tall glasses of iced tea.

"No, Mama, you promised me the other chicken story," I said firmly. I had to take this tack with Mama. She liked to have her stories coaxed out of her. She bit into a chicken leg, chewed thoughtfully for a moment. Mama still had most of her teeth, including the front ones, and a good dentist had replaced the few missing back ones.

"Just to honour the chicken we are devouring here," I added.

"You're the most aggravating young 'un," she answered. "I'll tell you a Cajun joke instead."

I settled. Her Cajun jokes were usually pretty good.

"It's about Pierre," she began. I nodded. Pierre was a familiar name in Cajun jokes.

"Well, Pierre was running this restaurant out in the bayous. He was featuring a kind of rabbit stew but some of the folks accused him of using horse meat in the rabbit stew and somebody brought it to the attention of the health inspector." Mama paused, picking off a too-crusty piece of fatty skin on her chicken leg. Mama didn't believe in cholesterol but she had her fat consumption limits.

"So the inspector came out and started questioning Pierre about his rabbit stew. Pierre finally broke down and confessed that he did indeed use some horse meat in the stew. 'How much horse meat, Pierre?' the inspector asked. 'Do you use more horse than rabbit?' 'Oh, no,' Pierre answered. 'I never use more horse meat … it's half and half,' I tell you. The inspector tasted the stew. 'Are you sure about those proportions, Pierre?' 'Oh, yes,' Pierre insisted, 'half and half. I use all the time in my stew, one rabbit to one horse. Half and half, right?'"

I laughed. "It sounds like my marriages," I said.

Ain't it the truth, I think as I turn over in my metal bunk, trying to shut out the cursed prison light, the heavy breathing of the woman sleeping on the floor beside me, the sounds of the radio from the cell of the weeping woman next door. I could complain about the radio since it's late, but I feel better knowing she has some company, some connection, even if its just a damn built-into-the-wall radio that seems to get only Rock 101. That's the only station any of the built-in radios in this prison will pick up. The other stations are so scrambled or so faint they are incomprehensible. Whoever is responsible for this maddening state of affairs should be forced to listen to Rock 101 day and night until they run screaming into the streets …

In spite of it all, I sleep. At least enough to feel reasonably awake when I get up in the morning, dress, eat and collect my papers, all the while navigating around the still-sleeping woman on the floor. It ain't easy. And it leaves me scattered. By the time I'm in the prisoner's box in the courtroom, I decide to hell with it, what do I need all these papers for, anyway? I know who I am, how I got here, what I was doing in the middle of that logging road. I don't need papers. I leave the prisoner's box, cross the floor and step into the witness stand. I do not swear on the Bible. I confirm. I am under oath.

I made the decision to represent myself in court back during the Clayoquot trials when my lawyer, Robert Moore-Stewart, brought to my attention the distinct advantage of self-representation. Judges hate having to deal with self-represented people, but this is simply because they have less control over them. Judges can threaten to call a lawyer before the law society if they think the lawyer impudent or aggressive, but a citizen is a citizen, accused or not, and is not necessarily bound by strict courtroom etiquette. Which means a citizen can disagree with the judge in no uncertain terms—without being downright disrespectful, of course—and the only risk is being rearrested in the courtroom. If you are already a prisoner you can gauge how much more time you are willing to serve for insolence to the judge. After my first Elaho arrest, Robert got my legal defence started in terms of paperwork and the early courtroom procedure, and then I took over my own courtroom defence.

But being your own witness on the stand is rather odd because there is no sympathetic person to question you, to bring out the good side of you, to stress your fine intentions. In my situation I must fend for myself. I launch into the story of my life. But if this judge really has read my Clayoquot book as he claims, he already knows the story of my life, of my political journey juxtaposed with my personal travels. One thing I didn't say much about in the Clayoquot book is my increasing alarm over the chemicalization of industry, including the logging industry. I hate to bring up this chemical business at my trial. It's an extremely emotional issue for me and this isn't exactly a sympathetic judge, in my opinion. But I feel compelled to mention it because researchers have identified a frightening link between cancer and artificial compounds in herbicides and pesticides that mimic estrogen. The female body recognizes these artificial estrogens as the real thing and either tries to use them, which disrupts the normal production and utilization of natural estrogen, or stores them in fatty tissue. Breasts are fatty tissue. Historically breast cancer has been primarily a problem for elder women. Now young women in their forties, thirties, even their twenties are being stricken. Like Barbara Ellen. She was twenty-seven when she was diagnosed.

I tell the judge how these pesticides and herbicides have been used routinely by the logging companies after clearcutting old growth forests in British Columbia. I stress that these artificial compounds that mimic estrogen sink into the topsoil and streams of the forests and into the water table below, how a certain amount of these powerful compounds become airborne and can be carried hundreds, thousands of miles away by the wind. We are all "swimming in a sea of artificial estrogen," as one American scientist put it. I talk about how these same researchers are also linking the fifty percent reduction in male sperm in the last fifty years to these same compounds. And how the rise of prostate cancer in men and the number of reproductive abnormalities in newborns—not only in humans, but in birds, fish and other beasts—are being connected with the artificial estrogens as well. The horror of it all washes over me afresh on the witness stand and I start crying. Mr. Flanz passes me some tissue.

I think Mr. Flanz is a kind man. Even though he is the prosecuting party here, I don't think he is actually enjoying his job at the moment. As he hands me the tissues, his dark eyes speak of his discomfort with the entire business of prosecuting grandma tree huggers. But when he actually starts cross-examining me, his demeanour changes abruptly. He seems to forget entirely that I'm a great-grandmother concerned with the future of everybody's grandchildren. I'm simply someone who has broken the law and this must be established beyond a reasonable doubt. He is doing his job.

I readily admit everything. Yes, yes, I stood on the road at Mile 21 for two whole days, I wasn't arrested until the third morning. Yes, yes, I tried to get the media interested. Yes, in fact that was my main intent, to bring the issue of the degradation of the Elaho Valley by Interfor before the public in as forceful a way as possible. Yes, oh yes, I am absolutely guilty of this, and I have no regrets …

After Mr. Flanz finishes, Les Mackoff, Camille Willicome's lawyer, cross-examines me, trying to rescue me somewhat, bless his heart. But I refuse the rescue. My own stance is to challenge the close cooperation—if not actual conspiracy—between government, the judicial system, the RCMP and Interfor. To do this I must be totally open, honest and clear in my intent and motives so that I cannot be accused of duplicity by this court or anyone else.

The judge does not question me at all. When I say I am finished, he excuses me. I know I have failed to touch him in a human way. It is through the courtesy of Robbie Fleming, who knows better than I how to get witnesses actually to appear, that I call Hugh Sutcliffe, one of the vice presidents of Interfor. I ask only a few questions of Mr. Sutcliffe and then sit down to hear the lawyers' questions. I will get another chance at Mr. Sutcliffe when the others have finished because I was the one to call this witness. As the cross-examination by the lawyers may take up the next court day, I will have the weekend to try to piece things together, to think more about Mr. Sutcliffe. If he was indeed in the Elaho, relatively close to the protesters' camp when things started to happen, what part might he have played in the events of that day? I head back to BCCW, hoping for a quiet weekend.

Chapter Six

I **have** had a hard week, and on Saturday, after the chores are done in our unit, I head out to the track. I love track time. Walking has always been one of my favourite mind-settling things to do. I need to try and digest what Hugh Sutcliffe has said so far on the witness stand.

The track is behind a ten-foot steel fence topped with barbed wire. Pretty hard to escape from this joint, although I've heard it's been done a couple of times. Not that I want to escape. I just want fresh air and sunshine. And to think undisturbed for a minute or two. I have advised my new roommate that I prefer to walk alone, and she's booting it around the track ahead of me. Frequently other inmates will fall into step beside me as I make my way around the track, curious to hear my story, wanting to tell me theirs. I usually oblige for a round or two and then excuse myself by telling them my legs are short, I have to walk slower, please go ahead without me. If that doesn't work, I bring to their attention that I'm seventy-one and I can't walk and talk at the same time. Failing that, I say I'm from Louisiana and have webbed feet and need the entire width of the track. Most take the hint on the first or second offering. It isn't that I don't want to talk to them. I do. But I can't get sidetracked from my mission, particularly today. However, I don't even get a chance to get into a thinking mode because I am bushwhacked by a young woman who is serving time for blockading an abortion clinic. She falls into step beside me, uninvited.

Surely I am an ally, she assumes. After all, I have so many children and grandchildren, I must be hard-line born-again, I must even be opposed to birth control. I laugh. On the contrary. Raising five daughters has sensitized me forever to the insidious discrimination against women on this continent, the second-class status we still enjoy in all of the important institutions of our society, including the churches. These institutions are male dominated because they reflect male values, and the notion that a woman should not be allowed the integrity of her own body is a male notion, a controlling one, and what right does this young woman have to try to tell another young woman what she may or may not bring forth from her womb?

Her reply is in essence a religious argument, and when I point this out to her rather heatedly she says, with such sweet Christian grace and patience that I want to shake her, that surely we can talk calmly about the matter. No, I say, we cannot. I am angry at the role the Christian churches have played in the subjection of women and, by extension, children. Look around at all the women in this joint, I say. Most are here because they have been abused as children, as young girls, and then they find themselves out on the streets because of the men who were supposed to have protected them. The average age of entry into prostitution is fourteen years, and many of these young women will probably die early because of men's treatment of them. And, I might add, some are second-generation addicts and drunks and thieves and hookers because their parents were violated by church pedophiles. Please, don't speak to me of religion. I make a sharp distinction between religion and spirituality. I am a spiritual being; I am not religious. Just as someone once remarked that school interfered with their education, I have found that religion has interfered, and continues to try to interfere, with my spiritual journey. "Go away," I tell the young woman. She goes.

I hate it when men, or women speaking for men and their institutions, try to equate passion with irrationality, and a calm manner with rationality. Some of the most heinous crimes in all of history have been discussed and decided on in a perfectly calm manner. Everybody has a right to be emotional. To show emotion, to be moved, to be angry—or even joyful, for that matter—is not irrational. Anyway, no one is more awash in a sea of emotion than the anti-abortion protesters when they are trying to block an abortion clinic. I can't afford to think about this right now, but it takes me a moment for me to shift gears mentally. Mr. Sutcliffe is waiting on my plate and he will take some pondering.

On the witness stand Mr. Sutcliffe had readily admitted that on September fifteenth he had a noon appointment with David Miller, operations manager at Interfor, at an appointed spot not far from the Lava Creek bridge and the campsite occupied by the protesters. He said he came in a helicopter with several of Interfor's stockholders on a routine visit. He testified that when he got out of the helicopter and went to the appointed meeting spot with Mr. Miller, Mr. Miller told him trouble was brewing: a significant number of Interfor employees along with Interfor's contractor's employees were extremely upset with the protesters and were heading down toward the protesters' camp. Mr. Sutcliffe said when he heard this, he told Dave Miller to forget about the meeting with him and the stockholders, just go, Dave, go. Then he got back into the helicopter with the stockholders and flew away.

At best, a cowardly thing to do, in my opinion. Dozens upon dozens of angry loggers were descending on eight unprotected people, one of them a woman, in an unprotected camp, and Mr. Sutcliffe, vice president of Interfor and presumably responsible for the behaviour of his company's employees in such a situation, simply leaves the scene. He flies away.

It seems to me that in almost any scenario I can think of, this would be an extreme dereliction of duty, certainly one that should warrant termination of employment. Mr. Sutcliffe, representing the top brass of Interfor, failed to provide firm direction or to indicate that physical violence against protesters would not be tolerated. He flew away, leaving the protesters at the mercy of an angry mob of men, numbering as many as eighty or ninety.

And while Mr. Sutcliffe has repeated ad nauseam on the witness stand that certain Interfor employees made very bad decisions, he was evidently referring only to David Haffey, Mr. Miller and Derek Sayle. He certainly has not, as far as I can see, referred to himself. Mr. Haffey has suffered a nervous breakdown and is in trouble with the court. Mr. Sayle has had some sort of trouble on the job. Mr. Sutcliffe says there hasn't exactly been a demotion of Mr. Sayle, but there has been some "reassignment of his duties." And Mr. David Miller, who was formerly the operations manager, now reports to another manager.

It seems that in their capacity as bosses in the woods, both Mr. Miller and Mr. Sayle have suffered to a certain extent for their decisions to remain at the Lava Creek bridge and not go down to try to stop the attacks on the protesters. Mr. Sutcliffe is adamant that these men made erroneous decisions and Interfor now just wants to go forward. But it seems to me that if Mr. Haffey, Mr. Sayle and Mr. Miller all made wrong decisions, then he, Mr. Sutcliffe, as vice president, the "big boss on the premises," made the most glaring wrong decision by not going down to the protesters' camp to stop the attacks. And yet he seems to be riding as high as ever with the company.

I will question Mr. Sutcliffe about this on Monday when he comes back to the stand. But before then I am again confronted with the old bugaboo of religion—this time in the prison setting itself.

◆

It is afternoon. A volunteer group has come to organize a softball game. I'm into this. I love to play ball, and it's a beautiful day. My inner child is delighted. Okay, kids, let's play ball! We are divided up into teams and spread out on the grassy yard inside the track. It's fun. Some of the inmates can actually play ball. Most can't. But some of the volunteers aren't exactly stars, either. There is a lot of laughing and good-natured hollering and then there's a break after a few innings and we all gather around the track steps for refreshments. And then, while I'm resting and enjoying my volunteer-sponsored juice and candy bar, one of the volunteer guys gets up and starts preaching the gospel and handing out religious pamphlets. I almost choke on my candy bar. I can't believe it. I carefully put down my drink and the remainder of my treat.

Yes, I was vaguely aware that this is a volunteer church group. But church volunteers do lots of things in the outside world, and if they don't preach at me I won't preach at them. But this is sailing under false colours. This is coming into a closed system and pretending to be something one is not. They are pretending to be bringing only recreation and treats out of the goodness of their hearts, but they have a hidden agenda. They want a captive audience. They want souls to save. They are not here because they want to be friendly and nice; they are here to indoctrinate us. They are not here for us; we are here for them. I take a deep breath and stand up.

"I object to this," I say to the man nearest me. He is a volunteer.

"You can't come to play ball with us and then preach to us." He is startled and perplexed at my outburst. "But why do you object," he asks? "Because I have religious freedom," I answer. "It is guaranteed under the Canadian Charter of Rights and Freedoms." He doesn't know what I am talking about, the concept of religious freedom obviously being a strange notion to him, and he asks but why wouldn't I want to hear the gospel? I assure him I have already heard it, my father was a minister. Wasn't my father a nice man, he asks, and I answer that compared to a lot of other Southern men I knew, he was downright outstanding, but that was beside the point. I push past him and leave. The other guy is still preaching.

I go back to my unit, but I am seething. I don't want to have my attention diverted by this, but at the same time I can't just let it pass. After a while I make a decision and march into the unit office to ask for a form to file a grievance. I am given a form. I take it to the dining section and sit down and start writing.

While I am filling out this form I try not to revisit all of my church-inflicted wounds on the subjects of race and abortion, women's place, women's duty, women's bodies, juxtaposed always with men's privilege. I was raised with Southern men who screwed black women at night and then kicked them and their entire race around by day while the church turned a blind eye to these doings and refused to come to the defence of black people, to lend a hand to help them get up off the ground. I don't even want to recall my own light of revelation, every bit as astounding as the biblical account of the light that blinded Paul, the unbeliever, on the road to Damascus, where God struck him down and called him into service. My own blinding light came through a black freedom rider named Stokely Carmichael, who came to the South to urge black people to vote and to fight for school integration. In a speech to fellow blacks he stressed the psychological damage done to black people by worshipping a white god: As long as black people prostrated themselves before white gods and thought the image of a white male was the image of the ultimate in strength and purity and power, he said, black people would never realize their own beauty, their own strength, their own power.

This insight struck me to the heart and I thought, oh my god, the man is talking about me, too. Although I'm white and I'm a woman, I realized that as long as women fall on their knees worshipping a male god we will never recognize the wonder and the power and the beauty of femaleness. And that is exactly why the entire Christian concept is male, why there is only God the Father, God the Son, and God the Holy Ghost, who must also be male because He impregnated Mary. Except for a brief nod to Mary for using her womb, the entire Christian godhead is male, including the devil and archangels. Stokely, my good fellow, I thought, you have inadvertently revolutionized me; you have struck me with the power of your words in a way you could never have foreseen. Yes, sir, now I see the light ...

No, I don't want to get bogged down by fuelling my present complaint against this church group with the heat of old angers; the new one on my plate is quite enough. So I finish filling out the form. After returning it to the office, I go to my room to work on the questions I want to present to Mr. Sutcliffe in the morning—but my roommate is working on her own trial preparation and has claimed the desk. I push back my sense of being violated. It's her desk, too. She has a right to be here. She is dealing with two different governments and has mountains of forms and papers. Lots of luck with that one, I think, as if dealing with one government bureaucracy isn't enough. I retire to my bunk with my own mountain of forms and papers.

But I can't concentrate. The radio is still on in the next cell and there is a constant babble of voices outside the door. I could go down and see if the library is open, but most likely it isn't. Officially it opens one hour a day for three days a week, two hours the other days, but since the library staff is composed of inmates, and we are a crisis-oriented group, the library may open at the appointed time or it may not. It may not open at all. I don't feel like pushing all the buttons on all the steel doors it takes to get down there to check it out. I'm tired. I push the pile of papers aside and lie down and close my eyes. I am used to sleeping with books and piles of papers, so their presence does not disturb me. But I don't sleep. For some reason, in my times of reverie in this place, my mind keeps going back to that last summer I had with my mother two years ago. I think it's because I'm not used to her being gone yet.

•

By the time Mama and I got Aunt Gladys home from the hospital two days after the aliens landed, we were all exhausted. Aunt Gladys was in her right mind—which was, in my opinion, a terrible place to be: bitching about everything. The visiting nurse was there frequently, which took the heat off me and Mama. But it only took three days for Aunt Gladys to gear up to her normal level of being impossible. After that, the nurse, who lived just down the way, said we were on our own except for the usual brief morning checkup for Aunt Gladys and an even briefer look at Mama's blood pressure once a week.

That afternoon the card game resumed. Aunt Gladys had done a lot of gambling in her life. In fact, she had been a bit of an addict before her heart started getting congested. Congested or no, she still loved to play cards or anything that involved shooting dice. She didn't like the slots very much, though they were better than nothing. But the way she acted you would have thought a million dollars was riding on our pitiful little games of thirty-one. Thirty-one was all Mama knew how to play so Aunt Gladys settled for that. I don't like card games of any kind. However, I thought the games were good for Mama and Aunt Gladys. Aunt Gladys would cheat once in a while, but on the whole it seemed to be going okay.

One morning a couple of weeks after Aunt Gladys had come home from the hospital—and I was thinking about going home myself— she got up complaining more than usual. Helen June, the nurse (so named because she was born in June and her mother claimed it was hell), decided to give Aunt Gladys a thorough examination. Aunt Gladys obediently submitted to Helen June's authority.

"You got your medicine patch on?" Helen June asked, frowning at Aunt Gladys' blood pressure reading. Helen June was a robust young woman in her thirties with long, thick beautiful brown hair that she tied back with colourful scarves. She was a single mom and sometimes on Saturdays she would take Tanya, her eight-year-old daughter, who also wanted to be a nurse, on her rounds about the countryside. Tanya was a good little thing, with her mother's lovely hair and brown eyes. She sat quietly on the couch in the living room, waiting for her mother to take care of the ladies. At this end of the woods people all knew each other, so Tanya's presence was welcomed; in fact, Helen June's father was an old acquaintance of Aunt Gladys'.

"Yes, ma'am, I do have it on," Aunt Gladys said in answer to Helen June's question. "Bug can vouch for that. I took my medicine last night when I was supposed to and Bug put on a fresh patch. Didn't you, Bug?"

Helen June wrote down this information in her notebook. She was still frowning. I glanced at Aunt Gladys. In truth, she didn't look well. She was five years younger than Mama but looked older. Mama radiated health. She looked like one of those pert little grandmothers in kids' storybooks, with puffy white hair and pink cheeks. And Aunt Gladys looked, at least at that moment, as if she could be the mean old witch in some of the same books.

"Don't pay any mind that my blood pressure is up," Aunt Gladys said crossly when Mama put fresh cups of coffee before her and Helen June. "Your blood pressure would be up, too, if you'd had the night I did."

"Couldn't sleep?" Helen June asked as she carefully placed all of her medical instruments and charts back into her little black bag.

"No. It was that Don Roy."

There was a small silence as Helen June, Mama and I all paused and looked at Aunt Gladys. Don Roy was Aunt Gladys' last husband. He'd been dead fifteen years.

"Did you dream about Don Roy?" Mama asked warily.

"Dream, shoot! He was in my room, right in my window."

Helen June paused in her business with her bag. Aunt Gladys now had everybody's undivided attention.

"You mean you actually saw Don Roy?" Helen June asked.

Aunt Gladys nodded, her bloodshot eyes wide, as she absently stirred the coffee in front of her.

"Yes, ma'am, I sure did see that very man. He was here, standing in my window, just as plain as day. He stayed there for most of the night."

Mama moseyed back to the stove and poured a second cup of

coffee for herself. Which was unusual; Mama rarely had a second morning cup. Maybe she figured it might be an extra long day.

"Oh, Gladys, you're just imagining things," she said, moving back to the table with her cup.

Aunt Gladys snorted. "I know what I saw. You think I wouldn't know my own husband?"

"Well, there might be a little room for confusion there," Mama said matter-of-factly as she drew back her chair. "You've had six."

I sniggered. Mama threw me a warning glance, but I couldn't help it. Aunt Gladys had been married six times, and none of her husbands was anything to brag about, in my opinion, including Don Roy. He was sexist and racist and he drank copiously. True, I've had a couple of sorry specimens of my own, but after the first two I learned that basically there are only two types of men, responsible ones and irresponsible ones. After two of the former type, I at least shifted gears. Aunt Gladys never did. It was because she had such a low opinion of women in general, I speculated. For her, the most wonderful woman who ever lived couldn't hold a candle to the sorriest man. Except for Mama. Mama was her lifeline.

"That don't make no damn difference, Bug," Aunt Gladys said indignantly. "Don Roy was the last and I was with him the longest. I'd know him anywhere. He was at my window last night, I tell you."

"Well, what did he do?" Helen June asked.

Aunt Gladys sipped her coffee thoughtfully.

"He rattled the blinds first," she answered after a moment. "Just to get my attention. And when he saw me looking at him he motioned me to come. And he just stood there, waiting."

"Gladys, that's crazy," Mama said. "Why didn't you call me or Betty?"

"Because every time I turned on the light he'd go away."

"Well, see?" Mama asked triumphantly. "That proves it was just something you were seeing in the dark." She turned to Helen June for confirmation of her theory. "Ain't that right, Helen June?"

I happened to glance across the kitchen counter into the living room. Little Tanya was still sitting quietly on the couch but her eyes were big and round and glued to Aunt Gladys' face. Aunt Gladys' story was scaring her. I turned to mention this to Helen June.

"Oh, yeah, Miss Gladys, you were just seeing things. People do that all the time when they're taking as much medication as you're taking," Helen June said, still trying to pacify Aunt Gladys. She paused to take a hurried sip of her coffee before leaving. Aunt Gladys placed her coffee spoon carefully on the table and looked at Helen June.

"Well, I'm glad you feel that way, Helen June," she said. "Because the only way I got Don Roy to go away and leave me alone was to tell him you ain't with your old man anymore and to go down and see you."

Helen June jumped out of her chair, sloshing her coffee into the saucer.

"What! You told him to come down to our place?"

"Yes ma'am, I did. Don Roy always told me you were the prettiest young thing to ever come out of the Delta. So I told him to go see you. And he left."

Helen June already had her bag in tow; she was on the move. Tanya, fully mesmerized, was yanked to her feet. "Tanya, honey, we have to go right now. Tell the ladies 'bye ..."

"But you didn't drink your coffee," Mama protested. Too late.

Helen June was out the door like greased lightning, dragging her child behind. We three elders were left sitting at the breakfast table. I nibbled on a cold biscuit, waiting for Mama's evaluation of the situation.

"Gladys, you shouldn't have talked about Don Roy in front of little Tanya. You know how young 'uns are. They believe everything they hear."

"Well, she can go ahead and believe what I said. I ain't lying. Don Roy wants me to come with him and I'm not ready. I'm not sleeping in that room anymore, either." She paused and looked over at me. "You sleep in my room," she ordered. "Or sleep over in the other place. I'm taking back the couch."

The other place is the mobile home next door that my brother Ray Allen and his wife Carol bought so kinfolk who come to visit Mama and Aunt Gladys would have room to spread out. Ray Allen and Carol lived in Arizona but spent some of the fall months here. I would have loved to spread out away from Aunt Gladys, but should anything happen during the night Mama might injure herself coming over to get me. So I would just have to accept Aunt Gladys' room.

There were advantages. Her bedroom air conditioner was almost as good as Mama's and she had an extension phone by her bed. I would be able to call my kids without worrying Mama. Mama didn't know the absolute seriousness of Andy's recent escape from the surgeon's knife. So that evening, after Mama and Aunt Gladys were both tucked in for the night, I called my children, one by one. I loved hearing their voices. Oh, the telephone is such a wondrous instrument! My children's adult voices only thinly cover their childhood trebles in my memory; for me they can never shed their sweet little boy and sweet little girl selves because they are so deeply embedded in my heart. Fie on voiceless communications. I want to hear the surprise, the anxiety, the affection in their voices. Hello, my darlings, I said. Well, I didn't exactly say that. That would embarrass them. But I talked to all that I could reach that evening, concentrating on Marian, the youngest. All of the others had partners looking after their interests, except Mike, who depended on the wilderness of the northern bush to take care of him. But Marian had suffered acutely from Barbara Ellen's illness and death and with me away, she was essentially on her own in the city. I called her last.

She was okay. Everybody was okay. Barbara, honey, are you okay, too, I asked silently as I hung up the phone. I wish I could call you, inquire about your journey. Wouldn't that be wonderful? But there is no phone number for you. Nevertheless, I felt comforted by talking with the others and got ready to retire. When I crawled into bed I tossed one of the baby blue satin throw pillows to the foot of the bed and was already half asleep before my head hit the other pillow.

But suddenly there was a rattling at the window facing Aunt Gladys' bed. I sat up, instantly wide awake. Was I hearing things? But no, the rattling occurred again. I strained forward, trying to see. The little night light on the dresser across the room cast just enough light for me to see a figure standing in front of the window. What was it? Could it be Barbara? Had I called her from the dead? I crawled down to the end of the bed, heart pounding, straining harder to see. No, it wasn't Barbara Ellen's slight, graceful form. The edges of the figure were blurred, but I could make out a heavy, somewhat stooped, definitely male outline. Don Roy?

A scream formed in my throat. My first impulse was to jump out of bed and run screaming bloody hell to the main wall light switch.

But that impulse was immediately hijacked by another. Whatever was happening at the window shouldn't have been happening. It was just another stupid phenomenon of one kind or another trying to get my attention when I already had so much grief and anxiety to deal with that at times I could hardly remember my name. I reached for another blue satin pillow and flung it as hard as I could against the window. The pillow hit the blinds with a soft but satisfying thud and fell to the floor.

"Don Roy, if that's you, you can just get the hell out of here, you jackass!" I yelled. "I don't have time to mess with your craziness!"

I waited, the nerve endings on my skin tingling with anxiety. But I refused to be totally spooked by such a poor specimen as Don Roy, dead or alive. Had I wakened Mama and Aunt Gladys? All I could hear was the blood coursing through my head. But the figure in front of the window seemed to have taken my displeasure to heart: It had all but disappeared. Could you really make a ghost disappear by shouting at it? I just stayed on the edge of the bed, waiting until the figure was no longer there at all and my heart slowed enough that I could crawl back to the other end of the bed. But then I thought of something. I picked up the remaining blue satin pillow and threw it against the blind, too.

"And don't you go down bothering Helen June and Tanya, either," I said firmly, not yelling this time. No need to yell anymore. I had him on the run.

I smile, remembering this episode as I lie in my bunk, waiting for my jail cell mate to finish with the desk. I wish I could make this judge disappear by shouting at him. But he's not going to go away. I have to try to play the courtroom game for a few more days and then it will all be over. In the meantime, I must try to think of some way to get the truth out of Mr. Sutcliffe. I feel sure he talked to either Duncan Davies, the president of Interfor, or William Sauder, chief shareholder of the company (who also happens to be the chancellor of the University of British Columbia). But how to get Mr. Sutcliffe to admit this? I must get up and make my bunk properly for sleep. Maybe I will dream the solution. But instead I dream of spiders.

Chapter Seven

Odd how the mind works. I went to sleep with lingering images of my mother, dreamed of spiders, and wake up knowing exactly what I want to ask Hugh Sutcliffe on the witness stand when I get to court this morning.

When the sheriffs come to get us for the early morning joy ride through the streets of Vancouver in the police van, leg-shackled and handcuffed, I am ready. The officers waiting to receive us at the courthouse cells greet us cheerfully and call me by name. We all know each other by now. It's almost like car-pooling to the office, greeting one's colleagues in a civil manner. Except for the leg irons and handcuffs, of course. And the interminable searches. While I wait in the cells for court to convene, I scribble down my thought.

From what I know of the workings of corporate hierarchies, which are similar to the hierarchies of governments (men not knowing how else to arrange anything, except in hierarchies), Mr. Sutcliffe would not have decided to fly away from a scene of potential criminal assault by Interfor employees and associates without first receiving authorization from someone higher up. But how to prove this? And even if Mr. Sutcliffe admitted on the stand that he had talked to Duncan Davies, president and CEO of Interfor, or William Sauder, chief shareholder and chair of the board, and they ordered him to fly away, what would that mean? If the bosses themselves had given the order to Mr. Sutcliffe to fly away despite possible impending criminal assault by

Interfor employees, would that mean the bosses had colluded in willful criminal negligence? I feel sure that Mr. Sutcliffe will never admit this, on the stand or anywhere else, but I will do my best.

Will my best be good enough? Mr. Sutcliffe is sitting there in the witness box nattily dressed, looking every bit the young up-and-coming executive. He seems quite sure of himself. Yes, he says in answer to my questions, the meeting between himself and David Miller was entirely a routine one. When he got out of the helicopter and went over to talk to David Miller, David told him there might be trouble brewing, as the men who were supposed to be working were in fact congregating to go down to the protest camp. He, Mr. Sutcliffe, simply said, "Okay, Dave, go. I won't keep you; we'll be on our way." Or words to that effect.

I feel a surge of contempt for this man. He is posturing as though he were a gentlemen, but in my opinion he is a coward. He allowed a bunch of angry, desperate men to form a mob and do what mobs usually do, which is beat up on somebody, or worse. And he simply left the scene. I ask him if he knew there were so few people in the camp. No, he didn't. Did he know there was a woman in the camp? No, he didn't.

"Sir, did you talk to Mr. Davies on any kind of phone while you were either on the ground or in the helicopter, before you flew away?" I ask.

He doesn't bat an eye. "I don't recall," he says. He doesn't recall? Now isn't that interesting. He can't recall whether or not he talked to the president and CEO of his company just minutes before he flew away from a mob scene involving his company's employees? Seems to me that anybody should be able to remember that. Just think. There's a potentially dangerous situation developing here as Mr. Sutcliffe chats with Mr. Miller. Mr. Miller knows it could be an extremely volatile situation. He informs Mr. Sutcliffe that he cannot stay to chat with him and several shareholders (one must assume that these are important shareholders, or they would not be toured by helicopter). He, David Miller, must go. This is not a typical event. This is a bizarre event, extremely abnormal. And yet Mr. Sutcliffe can't recall if he spoke to his president about the situation then or shortly after. Wouldn't he want to speak to his president about this? Wouldn't he be fired if he didn't report such a thing immediately? My stars! If Mr. Sutcliffe considered this a routine matter of little consequence, not important enough for him even to remember if he spoke to his president about it, if this is true and he still enjoys the good graces of Mr. Davies, then the company is so incompetent it should implode under the weight of its own stupidity. But I personally don't believe Mr. Sutcliffe considered it a routine or insignificant matter either then or now.

"Sir, you don't seem to know much about anything," I say with some heat. "I really can't think what Interfor pays you for."

But in fact I think I know one thing Interfor does pay Mr. Sutcliffe for and that is his absolute loyalty to the company. His company, right or wrong; his job, right or wrong; his career, his future, his … whatever. And that concludes my examination of Mr. Hugh Sutcliffe, vice president of Interfor.

This is such a frustrating business. And I'm angry at myself for being drawn into this court game. Mr. Justice Parrett has said more than once that the events of September 15, 1999, which are taking up so much court time, really have nothing to do with the outcome of our own cases. Then why are we doing this? Yet it's like a tar baby. I've put my hands on it and I can't put it down. And regardless of what Mr. Justice Parrett says about our own cases, there is a fundamental principle supposedly at work here, which is to try to get to the truth.

After court housekeeping the following morning, I am up again to question another witness, this time David Miller. Mr. Miller is a stocky, barrel-chested man with a gruff manner. He doesn't look quite as confident as Mr. Sutcliffe did. Mr. Miller says yes, he saw Mr. Sutcliffe because he had a meeting with him, and he cut the meeting short because he was worried about what might be happening at the protest camp, but no, he didn't actually go down there, he stayed at the bridge.

I give Mr. Miller over to the other lawyers to see what they can get out of him. As he is my witness, I will have the last crack at him before he is excused.

While Barney, Rick and I are rank amateurs at playing courtroom, I don't see that we do much worse than anyone else. That opinion isn't shared by Mr. Justice Parrett, especially where Barney is concerned. Judge Parrett seems to have fingered Barney as epitomizing all that is evil in the Elaho. Barney is irreverent, to be sure. In order to go against the established order of things, people frequently slop over into impoliteness. But there is no excuse I can see for Mr. Justice Parrett to exhibit such profound impatience with Barney. Could it be just because Barney said in a TV sound bite that Mr. Justice Parrett wasn't God?

When I get back to BCCW that evening, my desk is cleared. My roommate has been released. Glory! Now I can think undisturbed about Mr. David Miller. But hardly have I finished my frozen dinner when a woman comes to see me about the grievance I filed. She is in charge of volunteers, and she wants to know if I would be willing to meet with the alleged offending church group, along with the prison chaplain and herself, to discuss the matter. I agree. A meeting is set. After that lady's visit, the evening in the unit grows deliciously quiet—which means there is only one squabble over the cigarette roller and only one nearly physical altercation over using the unit washer and dryer.

Tempers flash so easily in here. Alliances can form, break apart, form again in the space of a couple of hours. Some inmates are locked down in their cells for misbehaviour; others voluntarily lock themselves down just to get away from the stressful interactions. Stress is rampant. One must take advantage of the quiet times.

I write letters, make phone calls to my children. The woman in the cell next door who cries half the night and plays the radio the other half has abruptly disappeared. Where to? Where do they go when they leave, these poor children of the great underbelly of capitalism? No, never mind, I won't inquire. The answer, if I get one from the guard, will depress me. Think about Mr. David Miller and the part he may have played in the great tape disappearance caper. But I don't want to think about Mr. Miller. I don't care abut him or the tape. It all seems so silly. Like cops and robbers, or cowboys and Indians, only the cops are on the same side as the robbers in this particular game and the Indians aren't playing at all. Maybe they're waiting to see who is left standing after the smoke clears.

Mama, you gave me some big answers about some things, I say into the void of my ever-lit cell, but you sure missed the mark on others. When I was little I asked you why it was that men were supposed to be the smart ones and be the heads of families when they did such foolish things as getting drunk and gambling and fighting. And you said it didn't matter, that God said men were supposed to be above women, it was in the Bible. What a pitiful answer that was, Mama. You were so smart about most things—plants, people, animals. But when it came to people you loved, like Daddy and Aunt Gladys, you just turned a blind eye.

I remember after Aunt Gladys was home from the hospital and well enough to play cards again, you wouldn't admit what a big ole cheat she was. We were playing thirty-one on a sweltering afternoon and we hadn't even gone two rounds when I caught Aunt Gladys cheating in an over-the-top manner. So I called her on it, and she threw down her cards in a fit and stalked out of the room. But not before flinging at me what she considered a supreme insult—that I wasn't a real Southerner anymore! I felt the gorge rise in my gut and my pulse accelerate with anger even though I knew this script by heart; we had played it out at least a dozen times. Why did this pitiful woman fill me with such rage? She slammed her bedroom door behind her. She wasn't afraid of Don Roy lurking in her bedroom during the day. No, Don Roy was a night crawler.

But I was shaken in spite of myself. Me, not a real Southerner anymore? Was that possible? But maybe by her definition of a Southerner, Aunt Gladys was right. I wasn't sexist, racist, an alcoholic, a gambler, a born-again Christian or a sex maniac who thumped the Bible on Sundays. Mama is my idea of a Southerner. She is warm and hospitable, generous and tolerant, despite her religion. But then I'm not much like her, either.

That afternoon two summers ago, Mama sat back down to finish her coffee. She looked at me reprovingly.

"Betty, Gladys is old," she said.

"So are you, Mama. Older than her."

"I don't care shucks about the card game. She does. It's important to her to win. If she wins then Gladys feels good."

"But, Mama … are you saying that you and I are just playing cards to let Aunt Gladys cheat so she can win so she can feel good?"

"I guess."

"But dope makes people feel good, too, Mama. For a little while. Why don't we just give her some dope and not bother with the cards?"

Mama drained her cup of the last of her afternoon coffee and then looked at me steadily for a long moment.

"She's already taking a right smart amount of dope," she said after a while. "It doesn't seem to do much good. Betty, don't be so hard on Gladys. She don't get much out of life except fooling around with that cat and playing cards. She don't read or sew and she can't do gardening anymore."

"But whose fault is it that she didn't develop any interests? All she wants to do is feel sorry for herself."

"Don't say any more bad things about Gladys. She's my sister. I raised her."

"And that's why she's so hateful to me. She thinks she's your kid instead of your sister, and that I'm a hated younger sibling."

Mama pushed back her chair. "Betty, just put the cards away. I have to write some letters. You find something to do, too, besides fault your poor old aunt."

Poor old aunt—right. But of course I didn't say that out loud. "I think I'll go over to Ray Allen's place and dance awhile," I said, gathering up the cards and chips. I felt the need for some vigorous exercise.

"Mind you don't pass out from the heat."

I was still fuming about Aunt Gladys' cheating and the way she spoiled her rotten cat, Sweetie. Sweetie may have started out as a decent cat but Aunt Gladys managed to pervert every decent feline instinct the creature might have had. But perhaps I was prejudiced. After forty-five years of dogs, cats, fish, birds, hamsters, guinea pigs, turtles and lizards, I was not fond of pets of any persuasion. Especially pets whose genes have been so mangled by humans that they scarcely resemble anything authentic in nature. It was only during the few years I spent at Cypress Bay in Clayoquot Sound that I developed a real understanding of animals.

The animals in the Clayoquot were wild. They made their own livings. They taught their young to make their own livings. They did not need me or any human. All they wanted from me was non-interference. The bears, otters, seals, raccoons, martens and cougars that lived side by side with each other, and for a brief time with me, were my neighbours—not pets, not inferior beings, not a substitute for children, but neighbours. We respected each other and kept our distance.

Sweetie knew I had her number, that she was, in general, a bad cat. But Sweetie didn't worry me half as much as Aunt Gladys' insistence that Don Roy was still hanging around. Because several days after Aunt Gladys swore she saw him at the window, Helen June brought up the subject again on a routine visit.

"Miss Gladys, you scared my Tanya out of a year's growth talking about Don Roy the way you did," she said after the poking and testing and prodding were over. I felt like trying to get on Helen June's patient list myself. Aunt Gladys was enough to stress out a tree sloth. But no, Helen June also looked stressed.

"Oh, I'm sorry, darling," Aunt Gladys answered immediately, all apology.

"Don't worry about it, Miss Gladys. It's just that Tanya refuses to sleep in her own room now. She wants to sleep with me all the time."

"Oh, Lordy. Well, it's a good thing you don't have a man sleeping with you anymore."

My God, how could the woman be so insensitive? Helen June looked positively stricken. She loved her husband, although I understand he wasn't exactly Mr. Joe Citizen-of-the-year.

"The point, Miss Gladys, is that I had just got Tanya used to sleeping in her own bed again. She was upset about me and Frank separating so I let her sleep with me for a while but now I have to train her all over."

"Well, I'm sorry, Helen June. You know I never had any kids of my own."

That was Aunt Gladys' stock excuse for being a selfish, self-centred clod. I think Mama invented that excuse for her years ago. Whenever Aunt Gladys' behaviour hit the totally unacceptable level, Mama hauled out the excuse that Aunt Gladys never learned to be loving because she didn't have children to teach her. I didn't buy it myself. I know lots of generous, life-affirming people who never had children.

It was terribly hot in Ray Allen's mobile home the afternoon I went out there to dance, but I got the little fan and the two big ones all going at once, creating a mini wind tunnel. Then I stripped down to my underwear. I kept an Elvis Presley tape in the tape deck. Elvis Presley had a tap-dancing soul: you could tap dance to almost everything he recorded. I started out with "Jailhouse Rock."

I can't remember a time when I didn't tap dance. I wasn't actually very good, but because I put so much energy into it, people thought I was good. Occasionally I was asked to perform for some benefit or other. Perhaps people liked to see me dance simply because the sight of a seventy-year-old woman in tap shoes is remarkable. But that day in my brother's mobile home I danced as I always had, for my own enjoyment. Tap shoes are a kind of percussion instrument, and I've always liked to make music of my own and feel the sheer joy of the flow of rhythm.

That's what I would really like now, I think, sitting at my desk in my jailhouse cell: to be able to tap dance, to work off some of the toxic stress produced by the trial and this prison. But I'm not allowed my tap shoes in jail. They could be a deadly weapon. I step outside into the common room and glance at the clock in the office. Track time is over but I need some exercise, so I step back into my cell and turn the radio on. Rock 101! My stars! There are only two volumes, high and low. I keep it on low while I do half an hour of exercise, then make it to the shower five minutes before lockdown. In bed, my thinking about Mr. David Miller suddenly clears somewhat.

It came out on the witness stand that Mr. Miller, who is the boss of both David Haffey and Derek Sayle, said that he, too, told Mr. Haffey to throw the tape over the bridge on September fifteenth. This muddies the waters about the tape even more. For why would Mr. Miller say this? He, like Mr. Sayle, wasn't helping himself with this unsolicited admission, and for these two to insist that they had instructed Mr. Haffey to throw the tape over when Mr. Haffey had testified that he did it without any outside influence is slightly bizarre.

And the thing about Mr. Miller's behaviour that caught my attention was that, unlike Mr. Sayle, who was somewhat cavalier about the entire episode, Mr. Miller appeared much more worried about committing such an infraction. Mr. Miller had got a lawyer soon after Mr. Haffey had broken down on the witness stand, and his lawyer apparently accompanied him to at least one meeting with a company official. The question of what Mr. Miller is really worrying about has been nagging at me. A possible answer begins to take shape in my mind. But how to prove it? Probably impossible. But I will certainly try tomorrow.

Chapter Eight

The defence lawyers in our trial are primarily concerned with proving their clients innocent, or failing that, convincing the judge that their clients didn't really mean or truly understand what they had done and should be sentenced to community service or electronic monitoring. As a last resort, a defence lawyer will plead for as little jail time as possible for their clients. My purpose here is different. For me the object is to bring the trashing of our public forests into the courtroom and, through the court, to the public. I am not as concerned with my particular sentence as I am with the publicity that could capture the attention of the people of British Columbia and convey to them the need for some immediate participatory democracy in our public forests. Because our objectives differ, the lawyers and I are taking different directions in our lines of questioning.

But it seems to me that if what happened to the tape is actually important, then all avenues should be explored. Rick McCallion, an environmentalist who loves to roam the woods, has been given leave by Mr. Justice Parrett to go to the Elaho to search for the tape, just in case it's still around somewhere. I feel sure in my own mind that the tape has been destroyed. I think David Haffey gave the tape to David Miller instead of throwing it over the bridge. And I believe the tape was in Mr. Miller's possession until Duncan Davies, either in person or through the chain of command, and either with or without consultation with William Sauder, ordered Mr. Miller to destroy it.

That's the only scenario that makes any sense to me. And that's where I will go with my questioning when it is my turn for a wrap-up with Mr. Miller.

When that time arrives in the morning, I ask Mr. Miller first about his knowledge of a possible telephone conversation between Hugh Sutcliffe and Mr. Davies on the day of the attack on the camp. Mr. Miller says no, he cannot recall if he talked to Mr. Davies or if Mr. Sutcliffe talked to Mr. Davies in his presence during their brief meeting. Again, this is a very odd response. A mob is forming, trouble is afoot, an unprotected protesters' camp is about to be attacked by employees of Interfor, and yet neither of these men, both of whom are directly affected, can remember if either of them spoke to the president of the company to inform him of the impending events and to ask for direction. These two men seem to remember the events of September fifteenth quite clearly until it comes to the question of whether or not Mr. Davies spoke to either of them on the telephone. Then they both seem to develop amnesia. They don't recall. I have raised eight children who have all lied to me from time to time and I know a fishy story when I hear one.

I am angry that these men swore on the Bible and are under oath. I remind Mr. Miller that he and Derek Sayle have both testified that they instructed Mr. Haffey to throw the tape over the bridge but that Mr. Haffey has denied this. Why would they have volunteered this information, and why did Mr. Miller get lawyered up if this was his only transgression? Was he perhaps covering up something potentially more serious?

Mr. Miller denies there was anything more serious. I ask him if the reason he and Mr. Sayle insist that they told Mr. Haffey to pitch the tape was because the tape wasn't pitched at all? That Mr. Haffey actually gave the tape to him, Mr. Miller? That he, Mr. Miller, would not have destroyed the tape without consulting with Mr. Sutcliffe or Mr. Davies? Oh, no, no, no. Never happened, he says. Under oath. On the witness stand. All he is guilty of is ordering Mr. Haffey to pitch the tape.

My company, right or wrong. I will sacrifice for thee, I will lie for thee, I will embrace dishonour for thee, I will die for thee ... the words of the old anti-war song from the Vietnam era course through my mind. Just substitute the word "company" for "country."

I can't shake Mr. Miller on the witness stand, and the judge is annoyed by my style of interrogation. I note that Mr. Justice Parrett doesn't question Mr. Miller, just as he didn't question Mr. Sutcliffe about anything. Other than remonstrating with me, the judge seems totally uninterested in why neither of these men can recall something as important as a telephone conversation with the president of Interfor while potentially criminal action was being planned by their employees. Yet Mr. Justice Parrett was very interested in questioning witnesses who might provide some testimony that would prove Barney Kern was running sophisticated guerrilla warfare in the woods and that we were all part of a vast, disciplined army. Oh, he would leave no stone unturned at that prospect.

But Mr. Justice Parrett doesn't pursue the truth in the same zealous way where Interfor is concerned, especially when it comes to subjects such as why these two men can't remember any conversation with Mr. Davies. In my opinion both of these men should have been questioned by the judge. Neither of them went down to the site where the protesters were being attacked, when it was clearly their duty to have done so. They deliberately stayed away from all the mayhem, thus giving tacit approval for the attack. They were given bad instructions, in my opinion, by Mr. Davies, president of Interfor, and now Mr. Miller, Mr. Sayle and Mr. Haffey were taking the fall.

But then, what do I know? I am not a lawyer. I am not a judge. I am not the head of a company. But I am a lover of this earth, and lovers are sensitized to the plight of the loved one. The Elaho Valley is being irreparably damaged by clearcut logging. The Elaho is at death's door and may not survive.

I go back to BCCW that evening with a heart heavy as stone. But as usual, brief conversations with my children cheer me. Sue, in Pennsylvania, is anxious about her two daughters, one twelve, one fourteen. Sue is a medical assistant at a street health clinic, which feeds her anxiety.

"I see so much, Mom. Young girls in trouble of one kind or another, girls as young as mine."

"I know, honey, but you can't get paranoid about your girls. You keep them busy in sports and they're both on the honour roll. You can cut them a bit of slack. Do you remember what you were doing when you were fourteen?"

There's a long silence.

"What's that got to do with my girls?" she asks finally. I laugh. Actually I'm not sure exactly what all Sue was doing when she was fourteen, because she spent a lot of time at her father's house. But I know enough about kids to know she was doing at least a few things that she'd prefer her own daughters not do.

I make a quick call to Rose Mary, who lives in Ucluelet. Katie Jo, her five-year-old, has seen me on TV. I had told the TV news interviewer that my older grandchildren thought it was kind of cool that I was in jail for standing in front of logging trucks, but that the little ones didn't quite understand. And that Katie Jo had told me to "just leave those trees alone, Grandma, and come play with me."

"Katie Jo told all of her little friends that you talked about her on TV," Rose Mary said.

"Well, I think I need to talk to you about her idea of why I'm in jail. She seems to think I'm here for molesting the trees."

"That's what all jailbirds complain about, Mom, that they're mis-understood," Rose Mary answers. Her family have all had summer colds, she goes on to report, and her husband's ancient cat finally died. And they're going camping on the weekend. Reassuring stuff. When I'm in jail I need to know the world is still turning outside. My daughter Margaret Elizabeth, who also lives in Ucluelet, is next. She has been redecorating the house upstairs. It's an old house, but she and her husband Andre have it looking great.

"Is there the same animosity?" I ask, wondering if people in the vil-lage are giving them a hard time because of my recent arrests. Ucluelet is a logging town. Or was. It's changing now, new people are moving in, doing other things, but after the Clayoquot blockades I was a pariah in the vicinity. Yet the animosity toward me felt by the logging community was never taken out on my children. When Bar-bara Ellen died, even people who seemed to hate me put aside their enmity and offered condolences. Some of their children had attended Barbara's ballet classes.

On a recent visit to Ucluelet, Margaret did something that touched me. We had been shopping in the village, and when we walked into the driveway the woman next door was outside in her yard. The woman's husband was a logger and she had avoided me since the blockades. Margaret saw the neighbour first and she switched over to my other side so she would be between me and the neighbour. Then she reached over and put her arm around my shoulders. When we reached the front door I turned and saw the neighbour looking at us. My daughter had been trying to protect me from any potential venomous looks by shielding me with her body. I thought that was sweet, especially as Margaret is somewhat reserved. Almost as soon as we were inside the house, the neighbour called and told Margaret that I was certainly welcome back in the community.

"No, Mom, things are fine," Margaret answers to my inquiry. "You're not big news here anymore. Besides, I'm taking a cue from Rose Mary. When people ask me if I'm from the same Camp family you're connected to through marriage, I say no, I belong to that other Camp family." She's kidding, I think.

Nobody's waiting for the phone so I quickly dial Marian. She has just wakened from a nap and is foggy. She is working very hard at school to maintain an A average and has just started a new part-time job. Her relationship is crumbling under the strain. She wants to tell me the dream she's just had.

"I was in the Arctic and I was trapped under this enormous sheet of ice. I couldn't breathe. I was dying. And suddenly this huge white bear broke the ice over my head and pulled me out. It was an absolutely magnificent white bear. I fell in love with him on the spot and told him I wanted to have his baby. Now what do you make of that, Mom? Just off the top of your head? Apart from the fact that I haven't slept more than four hours a night for weeks and there is no food in the fridge, and as I don't have time to wash clothes both pairs of my jeans are so stiff I think they got up and walked away last night because I can't find either pair."

"There's that pair you don't like with the bleach spot on the rear, in the bottom drawer in the closet," I remind her. "At least they're clean. And bleached."

"Thanks, Mom. Now what about the polar bear?"

Here we go again. I'm the dream interpreter. Sometimes dreams can be somewhat transparent; if not, I just make a wild guess. I do that now.

"Maybe the bear represents your studies," I venture. "You feel trapped because you are subconsciously fearful that you just can't learn enough fast enough, and then the white bear appears ... he's representing the sensation you get when you experience a breakthrough in your understanding of anthropology. Knowledge lifts you out of the sea of ignorance of what you're trying to learn. Does that work? You know, there's a white bear that lives on an island on the west coast. It's actually a black bear, but ten percent of the bears born on that island are white. The Native people call them spirit bears."

"Good grief! I've had a visitation from a spirit bear. One who has agreed to make me pregnant! You don't think it happened while I was dreaming, do you?"

I laugh. "Anything's possible. But you would certainly have some explaining to do."

"Especially to Henry. He hasn't accepted yet that I want to date other men. When are you coming home?"

I promise Marian I will be home soon. My sentence for my second blockade in the Elaho, the one with Suzanne, is almost over. I hang up when I see other women waiting for the telephone.

Now I have the meeting with the church people to get through. It takes place in the prison chapel. A short, dominant older man and a young, silent woman are representing the church. The prison chaplain and the woman in charge of volunteer services are also present. We all shake hands and sit down, but I come out swinging.

"I have the right of religious freedom," I say, displaying a copy of the Charter of Rights and Freedoms, "and because I am incarcerated does not mean I lose these rights."

"But you have the right to get up and walk away from the situation, which you did," the man from the church counters.

"I should not have to do that," I say firmly. "The places for recreation here are for the inmates, not for you. When I am in here this is home and you have no right to come in here and start preaching to me when I didn't invite you. You can do as other religious groups do when they come in here, which is to announce there will be a religious service and then whoever wants to attend will do so, but you can't use our playing field for a church service."

"Betty, we do so much good in here, we give hope," he counters, and I say, "What good you may or may not do in here is beside the point. There is only one point as far as I am concerned, and that is you are violating my religious freedom when you come into my space and start preaching to me without my consent."

We go back and forth for a few minutes. I refuse to let the focus waver from my rights. The man does all the talking. The woman from the church says nothing. The prison chaplain and the head of volunteer services interject from time to time. The upshot of the meeting is that the church group can have services in the chapel before or after a ball game, but they cannot use the playing field for evangelical services. I go back to my unit satisfied.

Still, the arrogance of the church group annoys me. In fact, the entire religious infiltration of the prison by church groups annoys me. Women prisoners are the most pounced upon group by religious evangelicals. It makes me wonder about the men's prisons: I have a hunch the men are not considered quite the captive audience the women are, simply because men as a group wouldn't tolerate it.

There are Bibles all over the place in here, but there is only one copy of the Charter of Rights and Freedoms and that's in the back of *Martin's Criminal Code*, kept on the top shelf of the library. I had to look for it, and the odds of most of these women ever finding the Charter on their own is infinitesimal. The odds of most of them even knowing about the Charter or that it might help them in some way is infinitesimal. If I had my way, for every Bible and religious publication placed in this prison there would be small handbooks on the Charter and easy-to-read articles on what the Charter means and might mean to women in prison. If we can have so many preachers here pitching their convoluted ideas and beliefs concerning hellfire and the here-after, why can't we have lectures on the Charter? It makes me angry that religious groups consider women in prison fodder for religious lectures on sin and repentance. Most of these women already feel like outcasts; why in the hell does society feel it's a good thing to rub salt into their wounds? And furthermore, why do we have a male chaplain in a women's prison?

But I have to put these questions on a slow simmer. My time in this joint is almost up. My sentence for my second blockade in the Elaho will be served by the middle of next week. Only a few more nights in this cell—a few more nights of thinking of Mama to lull myself to sleep.

◆

On the day of the card game blow up with Aunt Gladys, she and I had made up by evening, mostly because of the cooking. Mama and Aunt Gladys had cooked together for so many years their meal preparation was almost like a dance. Even then, in their nineties, and with Aunt Gladys practically at death's door, the preparation of the evening meal called for the utmost care and concentration. And even though Aunt Gladys might wish to send me on a trip to the moon during most of the day, as long as I was under her roof, my evening meal, as well as theirs, was a matter of importance. It called for co-operation. Of course I was assigned the lesser tasks of chopping and mincing and dicing, but even these functions required close supervision. So naturally Aunt Gladys and I had to speak to each other. And there was also the factor of Aunt Gladys' memory. She simply forgot what she was mad at me about.

Two days later, when Mama suggested having Geraldine and Sonny over to play cards, I agreed readily enough. I liked Geraldine and Sonny. They helped look after Mama and Aunt Gladys when neither my brother nor I was there. They let us know immediately if there was a problem, and they frequently had Mama and Aunt Gladys down to their house for family occasions.

The supper dishes were put away, the peach cobbler Mama had made earlier in the afternoon was cooling in the fridge, and Aunt Gladys was preparing a pitcher of iced tea. She was bright-eyed and chipper as she puttered around the kitchen in happy anticipation of having guests.

As the first hand of thirty-one was being dealt, Sonny was still apologizing for being behind schedule and arriving half an hour late. "One of the niggers who was supposed to be helping me move that trailer said he had to go home early and by God, he went," Sonny said matter-of-factly, throwing down a jack of hearts before picking up another card off the top of the deck. If Sonny threw down a high card, that meant he was holding a couple of good ones he could build on. I had a nine of hearts but if I picked up Sonny's discarded jack of

Betty Krawzcyk outside the law courts in Vancouver, British Columbia, where she represented herself in court.

Betty's mother and aunts in the 1970s (left to right): Aunt Sit,
Aunt Gladys and Mama.

Great-granny ready to return to jail to save Elaho Valley

By Andy Ivens
Staff Reporter

Betty Krawczyk considers herself a proud Canadian, a defender of democracy and a dedicated opponent of logging old-growth forests.

The 71-year-old great-grandmother has been arrested three times for her environmental activism in the Elaho Valley and has done stretches in jail in the last 12 months.

After making her final submissions to a B.C. Supreme Court last week in a criminal-contempt-of-court case against her, she began preparing herself for more time behind bars at Burnaby Correctional Centre for Women.

"What I am willing to do jail time for is a very simple thing," she told Justice Glen Parrett.

"I want the time I serve in jail for my own attempts to help preserve what is left of the Elaho Valley to be called by its true name — that I am in jail for blockading Interfor logging trucks — and not for contempt of court."

Krawczyk cited a recent case involving protesters in the Slocan Valley in which the judge who granted an injunction against the protest lamented the necessity of having to

Law Courts

BETTY KRAWCZYK
fought her case without lawyer

The problem, noted Justice Mark McEwan in the Slocan case, is that a person who is driven by his or her conscience into an act of civil disobedience does not wind up in court for his or her specific action, but rather for defying a judge's order.

Contempt of court, whether it is deemed civil or criminal, does not result in a person having a criminal record.

But at trial

decide what evidence he or she needs to hear.

A second aspect, which Krawczyk finds repugnant, is that the case turns the judge into an interested party, not a neutral arbiter.

The current state of affairs has evolved over the last few years because of a policy put in place by the Attorney-General's Ministry.

Krawczyk asked Parrett to throw out the case against her and eight other alleged contemners who are charged with defying his injunction last September.

Fourteen people were originally charged, but four pleaded guilty to the less-serious charge of civil contempt of court. Parrett gave those four jail sentences ranging from 24 to 56 days.

One American did not show up for court.

Of the nine remaining alleged contemners, Krawczyk, Barney Kern and Richard McCallion fought their cases without lawyers. The other six retained legal counsel, who will begin their final submis

Top Stories

ELAHO VALLEY LOGGING

Great-granny, six protesters found guilty of contempt

By Dene Moore
The Canadian Press

VANCOUVER — A 72-year-old great-grandmother arrested for anti-logging protests was one of several "designated arrestees" chosen for a calculated and manipulative campaign by environmentalists, says a B.C. Supreme Court judge.

Justice Glen Parrett found Betty Krawczyk and six fellow environmental protesters guilty of criminal contempt of court Thursday for violating a court injunction against blocking logging and road building in the Elaho Valley, near Whistler. One protester was found guilty of civil contempt of court while another was found not guilty.

"What can I say about Betty Krawczyk?" Parrett asked before he condemned the silver-haired crusader. "She at least has the courage of her convictions."

... doubt in her sincerity in sought in the ...

Groups such as the People's Action for Threatened Habitat and the Western Canada Wilderness Committee portray themselves as David facing down the forest companies' Goliath, he said.

"The reality is, however, very different," Parrett said.

These groups are highly organized, he ... llite phones to contact ... late Web

But Parrett said both sides have used violence and manipulation.

"The protesters are better trained, more controlled and more subtle in their attempts," Parrett said.

Parrett did criticize the questionable testimony of forest company officials and employees, one of whom admitted destroying evidence and lying to police.

He also urged an investigation into ... RCMP handled the attack on the

Krawczyk is scheduled to go to trial on Sept. 19 for her protest at the legislature.

Fourteen sheriffs guarded the courtroom after environmentalists and their supporters, disappointed at the ruling, began to shout at the judge.

Two of the protesters were rearrested. Joe Foy, of the Western Canada Wilderness Committee, said he considers the protesters heroes.

"It's hard to be peaceful when people are beating on you," Foy said outside the ...

Judge's order that logging protester must serve one-year term challenged

Defence counsel and B.C.'s attorney-general both contend the sentence is inappropriate

Headlines from newspaper clippings about Betty's arrest and trial.

Three generations of Betty's family in 1985. Back row (left to right): Aunt Sit and Betty's daughters. Front row (left to right): Betty, Mama (with great-grandchild), Aunt Gladys.

Mama in Louisiana.

Suzanne Jackson (left) and Betty serving sentences in the Burnaby
Correctional Centre for Women. (Photo courtesy Burnaby Correctional
Centre for Women)

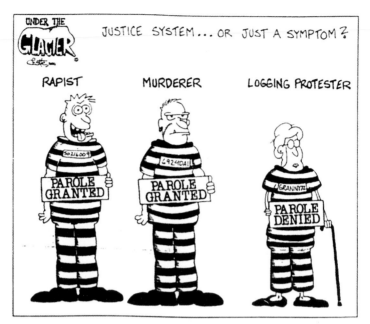

Editorial cartoon from the *Comox Valley Record*, November 15, 2000.

(Courtesy Bob Castle, *Comox Valley Record*)

Greenpeace postcard issued in support of Betty. The back reads: "The man on the right … took part in attacks against peaceful protesters in the Elaho Valley. But it is the woman on the left, Betty Krawczyk, a 72-year-old great-grandmother, who is serving a one-year jail term for peacefully protesting Interfor's logging of ancient rainforests …" (Courtesy Greenpeace Canada)

Protest in front of the legislative buildings in Victoria, British Columbia.

An impassioned speech at a protest in Vancouver. (Courtesy Marion Stoodley)

hearts I would never get another in the same suit from him, so I might as well discard my nine. I did, and drew another card from the top. But only part of my mind was on the game. The other part was on what I was afraid Sonny might say next. Or what I might say.

"Maybe he had a reason to go home early," I said.

"Oh, they always have a reason to get out of work," Sonny answered. "They just don't like work. They're lazy."

My heart hurt. That's where the pain hits me, right in my heart. It's almost like a physical assault when people I know, people who can be so good in so many ways, show such ignorant, vicious faces, like the one Sonny was turning to his wife. "Ain't that right, pudding?" he asked good-naturedly.

Her smile mirrored his. This was a second marriage for them both. They hadn't been married long.

"You're right, honey, you're always right," Geraldine answered, waiting for Mama to throw away a card. Geraldine looked over at me and smiled. "Betty, you mean well, but you been away from the South too long. You don't remember what it's like down here trying to deal with these niggers."

I lay my cards on the table, face down. My insides felt like the dry ice Daddy used to buy when I was a kid to put inside the ice cream maker. The ice fascinated me. How could anything be so cold and yet so smoking hot?

"All I know," I said slowly, "is that this town runs on the backs of the labour of black people. For a race who doesn't like to work, they sure do a lot of it. I haven't been anywhere in Vicksburg that black people aren't working: no service station, no grocery store, no restaurant, no office or service industry is running without the labour of black people. If one of your white workers asked to go home early, would you then describe all white workers as being shiftless and lazy?"

There was a sudden silence. Everybody looked at me. The silence grew.

Aunt Gladys started fidgeting with her poker chips. She had the annoying habit of clinking them against the tabletop. "Can we play cards?" she asked plaintively, sensing that her gambling evening was about to be ruined.

"Betty, you just don't understand," Geraldine said. "You're not a real Southerner anymore."

"I already told her that," Aunt Gladys snapped, turning to Mama. "Didn't I, Bug? Didn't I tell Betty that very thing?"

"Yes, you did," Mama answered slowly, looking past her sister to Geraldine. "Geraldine, I'm a real Southerner," Mama went on, in careful, even tones. "I been in the South all my life. And I feel the same way Betty does."

The dry ice around my heart began to melt. I knew what Mama was risking by backing me so unequivocally in front of Geraldine and Sonny. Mama was ninety-five years old. She didn't drive, she had never driven. Neither Ray Allen nor I could be there with her all the time, and the grandchildren only came for brief visits. When none of us was there, Mama relied on Sonny to get to the doctor, the grocery store, the pharmacy. Mama felt responsible for Aunt Gladys, and my aunt's medical needs were ongoing and constant. In a few weeks I would be back in Canada, leaving her and Aunt Gladys in Geraldine and Sonny's hands.

The silence grew very long. Geraldine threw Sonny a questioning glance.

"Damn it all, I just want to play cards!" Aunt Gladys shouted.

"All right, Gladys, calm down, we'll play cards," Sonny said, giving a funny little forced smile. "And we won't talk about the niggers."

"They're not niggers," I said. "They're black people."

Sonny's eyes held mine for a moment but then looked away. He was obviously thinking. So was I. Could Sonny be considering the financial arrangement between him and Geraldine and Aunt Gladys concerning the mobile home? The deal where Aunt Gladys was to leave the mobile home to them after her death, along with her old car, a valuable antique record collection and all her diamond jewellery? Did any of this enter into his thinking? That if he was rude to me and Mama we might try to contest, after Aunt Gladys' death, what she had already given to them on paper? And was Mama banking on Sonny thinking of that?

"Have it your way," Sonny said briefly, his grin broadening. "Let's play cards."

After Geraldine and Sonny left that night and Mama was ready for bed, I went into her room. She was sitting in her big easy chair with a pen and pad in hand, going over a list of items we needed to buy at the store the next day. I sat down on the footrest across from her. Mama loved the colours pink and lavender. The soft light from the pink lampshade over her head bathed her white hair and lavender bathrobe in a rose glow as she contemplated the list. As I waited for her to finish, I looked around the room, my gaze lingering on the familiar objects: the many framed photographs of children, grandchildren and great-grandchildren on the dresser and walls, the soft, purple-flowered bedspread with matching curtains, the sliding doors, the electric piano, the hymnbooks, her sewing machine. I always felt safe in Mama's room.

"Aren't you going to bed?" Mama asked.

"Yes, but I want to tell you …" I paused. I didn't know exactly how to phrase what I wanted to say.

"That you think I'm wonderful?" she asked, her tone playful.

"Yes. Exactly that."

"Well, I'm not. I just do the best I can every day."

That was her stock answer, her recipe for the happiness and salvation of the universe.

Chapter Nine

My discharge date takes forever to roll around, but finally I am allowed to gather up my belongings, call friends for a ride home, go through the lengthy process of one final search of my person and clothes and books, one last goodbye to the staff in the discharge unit. I walk out the back door of the building into the bright sunshine and the arms of my friends. Oh, life can be sweet! Even the downtown east side of Vancouver looks good as my friends escort me to the townhouse gate with all the belongings I have accumulated in prison.

Just as I am swiping my card through the electronic gate system, a young woman passes who was released from prison shortly before me. We had talked a bit in prison; she had told me of her early life in a logging town. She is so stoned as she passes that she doesn't recognize me. I stare after her for a moment. She has obviously been using drugs nonstop for several days. Her gait is shambling, her clothes soiled, her hair a mess. Ah, yes, I'm home.

Jail time, the structure of jail time, recedes almost instantly once one walks out the gates. Now I do not have to be anywhere at any particular time unless I care to. I do not have to stand outside my cell to be counted, rise at a certain time, go to bed at a certain time, eat at a certain time, do certain chores at a certain time or go outside and exercise at a certain time. I do not have to wait my turn to make phone calls, to shower, to launder my clothes or to get my mail.

There is, however, the stress that was in abeyance while I was in prison, the stress of knowing that I am responsible for everything in my immediate environment: keeping the house clean and in order, food shopping, cooking, cleaning the bathtub and paying the bills. Fortunately Marian, with whom I share the apartment in Gastown, shares my housekeeping standards, which are fairly low or we would not survive living together.

We've discussed from time to time the possibility of hiring an occasional cleaning woman, but we can't decide exactly where she would clean. Our books and papers are everywhere. The entire apartment is like one big filing cabinet, except that nothing is properly filed. What we really need is a secretary, and who can afford that? The number of meetings we each attend is ridiculous, she with Save the Children and school, me with environmental and women's groups. But most of my commitments will have to wait because I must compose my final arguments to Mr. Justice Parrett.

There is no good place to write. Out in the Clayoquot I had no electricity and wrote everything by hand, which was tedious. Here in Gastown, televisions blare next door, traffic noise abounds and there are the added attractions peculiar to the Downtown Eastside. In the Downtown Eastside, people also live in the alleyways.

I have been trying to concentrate on writing since eight-thirty this morning. It is now ten. In the alley below my window an argument between a man and his girlfriend has been continuous, with only five- or ten-minute breaks, since six this morning. They are both either wired or drunk or a combination thereof. I keep thinking that one of them will eventually pass out, or that someone from their own community will intervene. It is useless to call the cops unless someone is convulsing or bleeding profusely. It is equally useless to yell down at them to go home. They are home.

"Fuck you, you asshole. I know what you did, you motherfucker."

"You're just a crazy bitch. You don't know anything, you fucking whore ..."

"You stole my tobacco. I know that. You stole my tobacco right outta my pocket ..."

"You dreamed that, you crazy cunt. I ain't got your tobacco ..."

"Then you smoked it all, asshole ..."

I decide it's coffee time. I make my way downstairs to the kitchen. When the coffee is ready I take it into the small living room connected to a patio balcony. The townhouse is brand new. It's tucked behind a huge new apartment complex that faces Cordova Street. The arrangement makes the four townhouses seem semi-secluded. In the master bedroom, windows line one entire wall and climb all the way up to the soaring cathedral ceiling. I gave that room to Marian, as she writes and studies and sleeps all in one room. The rent on this townhouse isn't cheap, especially given its location in the heart of addictsville. One block away in one direction are the cobblestone streets of Gastown with their expensive tourist shops; go two blocks the other way and you're in Pigeon Park, one of the most popular shooting galleries in east Vancouver.

How did we come to live here? I'm not sure. Marian's job is concerned with street children, but we moved here before she started that job. And while she writes about the Downtown Eastside, she was also doing that before we moved here. So was I, after a fashion. But suburbs never seemed a reasonable option to me. They offer neither the conveniences of the city nor the comforts of the country. But the Downtown Eastside? I guess I live here voluntarily because it keeps my revolutionary edges honed. Every day I see the dark underbelly of corporatism: the crushing of people by machines and technology; the value system that throws people away unless they fit the corporate mould; the waste of human lives for lack of a fair allocation of resources. As we did not consciously choose this neighbourhood, the only conclusion I can come to is that it chose Marion and me. And as long as the alley is reverberating with domestic quarrels, I will go shopping in Chinatown, a couple of blocks away.

I love Chinatown. I even enjoy the merging of all the Chinese food smells, which puts off some of my less earthy friends, accustomed as they are to the pale, delicate scent of plastic wrap. I buy greens in Chinatown that closely resemble turnip greens. The peppers and celery are crisp and fresh. So are the carrots. And then, as is my habit, I choose an unfamiliar vegetable or fruit. Just one, to taste. Starfruit is today's choice. Actually, I've had this before and I know I like it, so I take two.

I walk home along Powell Street with my backpack bursting with fresh vegetables and tofu goodies. This part of the neighbourhood is definitely in transition. There are some trendy, expensive restaurants and upscale renovated apartment buildings. So I dawdle, looking at the buildings and dodging the occasional drunk. It's still morning so the serious panhandlers haven't emerged yet.

By the time I get home with my treasures, the argument in the alley has gone somewhere else or died from exhaustion. After putting the groceries away I beat it upstairs to resume my address to the court. But I need a little nap first, just a wee one. Last night I read far into the night, and then the lovers' quarrel in the alleyway awakened me early. Now I fall asleep immediately. And dream of my mother. That she is calling me. The way she did two years ago when Aunt Gladys fell.

◆

It was a week after the card game blow-up that Aunt Gladys fell. I was over in the other mobile doing my daily Elvis Presley imitation to his rockabilly music. I kept the volume low so I could hear Mama should she call me, but that day I could have heard her even had Elvis been cranked up all the way. Mama's voice was shrill with panic when she yelled at me from the back door.

"Betty, come quick! Gladys fell!"

I kicked off my tap shoes and raced barefoot across the yard to Mama's side.

"In there!" she cried, pointing.

Aunt Gladys had indeed fallen. She was sprawled on her back in the middle of the kitchen floor. As soon as she saw me she started struggling to get up by herself. I knelt down to restrain her.

"Aunt Gladys, stop wriggling around," I commanded. "You might have broken something. Are you in pain?"

She grimaced up at me.

"Hell, yes, I'm in pain, you ninnycompoop. Can't you see I'm in pain? Just help me up."

"Betty, help her up," Mama said firmly.

I looked up at my mother. "Mama, she says she's in pain. She shouldn't be moved until we can get an ambulance out here ..."

"Damn it, Betty, I don't need no ambulance!" Aunt Gladys hissed at me. "Just help me to my feet."

I appealed again to my mother's superior common sense.

"That's what she wants, Betty," Mama answered. "Just help her up."

"Even if it kills her?" I asked, shocked at Mama's response.

Mama's eyes held mine. "Even," she answered.

Hellfire. I hated what was happening. Against my better judgement I lifted Aunt Gladys up high enough for her to grasp the seat of one of the kitchen chairs. From that leverage point I managed to hoist her upright with Mama helping to hold her steady. Aunt Gladys hadn't yet gained back the weight she had lost in the hospital, so I was able to half carry, half drag her over to the couch. She slid out of my grip and crumpled into a heap on the couch, moaning and cursing softly. No grandstanding here. The woman was in agony.

She made a move to turn over on her side but stopped midway, tight-mouthed and white-faced. Then she gave a piteous little cry as she tried to straighten out her left arm. Could a broken rib have punctured a lung? Was the arm broken?

"Aunt Gladys, at least let me call the doctor," I persisted. "There's no point in just enduring pain."

"Hush about it. When I want to see a doctor I'll tell you."

I turned to Mama in total exasperation.

Mama shook her head. "Just leave her. I'll get some wet facecloths."

A lot of good, that. I sat in the rocking chair next to the couch and watched Aunt Gladys try to turn onto her side once again. She didn't make it. She tried again and again. Was she crying? Finally she raised one hand in a helpless gesture toward me.

"Betty," she gasped. "Go ahead. Call that damn ambulance."

I scurried to the phone. The ambulance was there in a surprisingly short time considering the distance. I followed it to the hospital in Aunt Gladys' car, glad at least that I had managed to persuade Mama to stay home, as Aunt Gladys' old buggy's air conditioning had given up the struggle entirely.

At the hospital I ferried Aunt Gladys around from room to room in a wheelchair. She was examined, X-rayed and given magic potions, and finally we were parked in a separate room to await the doctor's arrival.

"I want a Coke," Aunt Gladys announced as soon as the nurse had left the room.

"There's no Coke machine up here," I answered. "These are just doctors' offices. Do you want me to go down to the cafeteria?"

"No. I don't like being alone in this crazy place. People steal your clothes."

"I know," I agreed, trying to mollify her. But the funny thing is that the last time Aunt Gladys had been in this hospital, her clothes did mysteriously disappear. At discharge, when the nurses couldn't find her clothes, I went to a nearby discount store and bought her a cheap new pair of slacks and pullover rather than drive all the way home and back.

Not that many of Aunt Gladys' clothes were actually worth stealing, except those Mama had sewn for her. Everything else was at least forty years old, which means if they weren't so shabby they'd be back in style. And she used to be so vain, this woman. For most of her life her looks and her clothes had been the most important things to her, after her men and her restaurants. When I was young and mad at her about something, she'd give me a hurt look and ask quite seriously, "But Betty Boopy, don't you love your pretty Aunt Gladys?"

The answer was no, then and now. But back then her hair was long and velvety black and beautiful, and her mother's Cajun blood was reflected in her dark, compelling eyes. She bubbled with laughter and men stopped to see what she was laughing at. Unfortunately, Aunt Gladys had a distinct taste for losers. Now the only thing left that reminded me of the beauty she had been was her long red finger-nails, which were presently clutching at my arm.

"I saw a water cooler in the front office," I said. "I'll get you a glass of water."

She recoiled in horror. "You know I don't drink water. What's the matter with you, girl?"

"Aunt Gladys, your mouth is so dry you can hardly swallow. And there is no Coke, no juice and no whiskey in this office. I'll bring the water."

When I returned with the water, I learned the nurse had come in and given Aunt Gladys a shot for pain. She was already dozey. I held the glass to her lips. She pushed it away.

"I'm not crippled," she said indignantly.

"But your arm—"

"Never mind my arm. I can certainly hold a glass."

I put the glass of water into her hands. She stared down at it for a long moment.

"Drink it," I commanded.

Aunt Gladys looked up at me and then back at her glass. "Hello water," she said softly and then drained the glass. I went back for a refill. When I returned, the doctor was there.

The doctor announced that Aunt Gladys must be readmitted to the hospital. She had a fractured rib, and while the arm wasn't bro-ken, it was bruised. However, the main thing the doctor was worried about was the distinct possibility of some complications around Aunt Gladys' hip implant.

After we plodded through all the necessary paperwork, Aunt Gladys was settled into a private room. The necessary paperwork was formidable, as Aunt Gladys was not on Medicaid. She had too much money in the bank to qualify for Medicaid but it would not be enough to pay the doctor and hospital bills she was rapidly incurring in her old age. Before she died, they would get every cent Aunt Gladys owned.

The process of checking an elderly woman without Medicaid into the hospital is uncivilized. America should hang its head in shame at not having a universal health care program. Like Canada. Like all civilized countries. Sweet Jesus, how I despise the Republicans and the American Medical Association for fighting against such a basic right.

Three hours later I was on my way home. The afternoon heat had hit its most hellish stride. No air conditioning in the car, but I was reasonably prepared. My own blood had thickened, as they say, from my long residence in more northern climes, and I could easily pass out in the car while waiting for a stoplight to change. So I had a tall paper cup full of water and ice perched at the ready, in the cup holder below the dashboard. When I stopped for a red light I simply poured some of the ice water over my head. It worked fine. And it restored my senses enough to realize that I had to do something immediately about the air conditioning.

On the way home I stopped at Sonny's place. Sonny would inherit the old car after Aunt Gladys died, so he agreed to take responsibility for the air conditioning that very evening, and he even dropped me at Mama's door. There was no reference to the card game earlier in the week.

Mama greeted me, her face screwed tight with anxiety. But she relaxed when I assured her that Aunt Gladys' injuries weren't life-threatening. As Mama looked pale and drawn herself, I insisted she go take a nap. And then I also sought refuge in the coolness of Aunt Gladys' bedroom.

I actually didn't know if Aunt Gladys' injuries were life-threatening or not. And I certainly didn't tell Mama that the doctor took me into her private office before I left and strongly recommended that Aunt Gladys go into a nursing home once she had left the hospital. I would wait a while before I dropped that little bombshell. I'd lived long enough to learn that some problems solve themselves. But if Aunt Gladys did have to go to a nursing home, something would have to be done about Mama. She couldn't stay on in the mobile home alone. Unless she had a companion, she would have to move back to Baton Rouge, into her old apartment in my sister Doris' house.

Doris had been dead for fifteen years. Carter, her husband, had never really recovered from the shock, but he was well taken care of by his son Jean and Jean's wife. Their other three boys were around, too, with their families. Mama's apartment was kept empty except when used by guests, in case she should need it. And in the days that followed, she did.

◆

My nap is over, I am wide awake now, back in Gastown and conscious of all the tasks I have set myself to complete before day's end. First, there is the address to the court that I must compose. With a cup of coffee at my elbow, I open up my word processor.

"Sir," I begin. I always call the judge "sir." The lawyers and court clerks address the judge as "My Lord." "My Lord" is just too foreign to my tongue, too foreign to my notions of democracy.

"Sir," I say aloud, trying to conjure up Mr. Justice Parrett's coun-
tenance. When I imagine him before me, it helps me concentrate on
what I want to say. The words begin to flow.

"Sir, Hegel, the German philosopher, said that the truth is in the
whole. Even if we assume that all that has taken place in this courtroom is the truth, it is still only half of the whole. The other half of
the truth is in the Elaho Valley, in fact, *is* the Elaho Valley. But I can't
bring the smells, sights, sounds and touch of the Elaho and its creatures into this courtroom because there is no legal avenue to do so.

"You have not allowed the defence of Justification. I can find no
comfort in any of the court rulings, either past or present, in civil or
criminal contempt of court proceedings that would actually allow an
investigation of the destruction of B.C. public forests by logging companies. It's as though this destruction is beside the point as far as the
courts are concerned, and yet it is the very destruction of the Elaho
Valley that has brought us all together here in this courtroom. Sir, I
have been in this courtroom for so long I feel I know you better than
I do a couple of my husbands, and yet the underlying reason for my
being here cannot, under the instructions of the Attorney General
and this court, actually be examined and used for defence."

Is it too wordy? Too flip, that part about knowing the judge better
than a couple of my husbands? But I have learned from my writing in
general that the first few paragraphs must grab attention. In fact, the
first sentence had better be pretty good. And regardless of the quarrels I may have with Christianity and the writers of the Bible, the
opening line is an attention grabber. "In the beginning, God created
the heavens and the earth." Now, that's what I call a beginning. But I
must get on with this.

I need a bridge here. What was it that John remarked recently about positives and negatives? John, my next-to-last husband, who is a mathematician. Yes, that's it. I will throw in a little positive and negative stuff here.

"Sir, you have stated, as have other Justices, that we are here because we have deliberately placed ourselves in this negative position. And there is certainly an element of truth in this. But there is another truth about the matter. The destruction of a forest is also a negative thing. When protesters take a negative stance to this original negative thing then you have a negation of a negation and in mathematics and in the real world two negatives make a positive. As an anti-logging protester, sir, I know I am a positive, as are the other contemnors, and no amount of jail time could convince me otherwise. But as the Elaho Valley cannot be brought into this courtroom then I consider myself her representative, just as the others who are here defending her are also her representatives."

Does this make sense? Is it too melodramatic? Leave it, but get more focused.

"Sir, Interfor shrugs when they cut down thousand-year-old trees and ask 'So what? They are a renewable resource, aren't they? Other trees grow back just like the thousand-year-old ones we've cut down, don't they?' And yes, they might grow back. In a thousand years. Maybe. Or maybe not. Trees like the ones that are being cut down in the Elaho Valley may never grow again, ever, because the soil conditions are being altered along with the protecting canopies, the wildlife and the very climate of the valley itself. Interfor knows this. And they don't care. And neither do they care about their much-touted second-growth tree farm trees that are genetically altered, chemically poisoned and grown on depleted soils. These trees won't bring diddly squat in the world market, not in ten years, twenty years, or even thirty years."

Oh, yes, now I'm getting into it. Interfor propaganda sings the song of "Oh, yes, a tree is a tree, one tree equals another, really, can't you see that, you dear, busy, gullible citizens of British Columbia who have allowed us hitherto unlimited access to your public old-growth forests, can't you see that one tree is as good as another? Why are you worrying your little ole heads about the rape of your forests now? Go back to sleep. Everything is just fine …"

Oh. Oh, how I despise them! My blood is pumping now and my brain circuits are striking fire.

"Sir, Third World countries are investing in incredibly fast-growing Eucalyptus trees and other species of trees that can be brought to maturity in an amazingly short time. A Eucalyptus tree in a warm climate comes to maturity in eight to ten years and is one of the biggest trees in the world. It makes excellent pulp and reasonable building materials, and Third World Eucalyptus is beginning to flood the pulp market on this continent as we speak. British Columbian second- and third-growth trees will never be able to compete in world markets with the World Bank-financed Eucalyptus being grown so fast and so very cheap. And Interfor knows this. And when Interfor gets all the valuable old growth it can from the Elaho Valley it will cut and run, as it has in every other logging area it has devastated, leaving the second-growth tree farms they have mouthed like a mantra to rot or ruin on their own. So how is it that citizens like me who so vehemently protest the cruel theft and destruction of the Elaho Valley forest can't bring the issue of this theft, this destruction, into the courtroom as a proper defence?"

This is what is so maddening. Once one is arrested under an injunction one automatically falls into the contempt of court category, and that is what one is tried for, not for the infraction one committed. The logging companies, with the help of the Attorney General's office and the justice system, have made it impossible for citizens to protest the murder of our old growth forests without being charged with contempt of court. It is as though Interfor and Mr. Justice Parrett and the Premier and the Attorney General are all dancing a quadrille while the ancient trees are falling and the forest animals are being driven to extinction by the annihilation of their homeland. But I must continue.

"Sir, I have come to the conclusion that it is because the law, as it is written, seems to be rather excessively concerned, in my opinion, with property rights. And because of the law's extreme sensitivity to property rights, these tree farm licences given out have come to be regarded as property rights by the courts instead of as being merely leasing contracts. And by providing some jobs and by taking advantage of general public ignorance about how destructive their logging practices actually are, Interfor, along with other international logging companies, has accrued to itself all of the advantages of private ownership of vast areas of British Columbia with none of the responsibilities of land ownership."

I hear Marian's key in the lock downstairs. She has had a trying day—exciting, but trying. She has signed a contract to write a government report on aboriginal youth and the sex trade. It will be a challenge. This is the area in which she has been working with Save the Children, working to make a difference. Nothing is more exciting than that. But she needs to de-escalate the excitement of the challenge because she also has an important university paper to write. I pamper her with smoked oysters and a glass of wine while I'm stir-ring up a pot of Chinese greens.

While the greens are simmering I reheat yesterday's corn bread and two fresh salmon patties from the fish market. Wild salmon, I was assured in broken English by the Asian woman who made the patties. Would it be, could it be, wild salmon? Most likely not. Why did I buy the patties if I wasn't sure? Because there is no place in our neighbourhood where you can be sure. Worrying about whether the fish is wild or farmed is the least of most people's worries who live here: Whatever presents itself to be eaten will be. I hear Marian turn on the TV in the living room. It's time for *The Simpsons*.

Marian loves *The Simpsons*. She wants to do her master's thesis, she says, on *The Simpsons*. Some drivel about postmodernism and the social paradigms as played out by each member of the Simpson family. She will, after all, be concentrating on the media in her graduate social anthropological studies. The truth is, she just loves *The Simpsons*.

Dinner over, Marian retires to her private hole in the universe, I to mine. I must finish the first part of my final arguments to the court. I address the judge about the book entitled *Falldown*, published by Ecotrust and the David Suzuki Foundation. This book traces the history of the first tree farm licences and describes how smaller, B.C.-based logging was nudged out of the tenure race to leave a clear field for the largest, most ruinous of companies, and how this was a deliberate political decision by the government of the day. I conclude this section with the following:

"Sir, in my opinion, this is tantamount to giving legal and govern-mental approval that allows to this day multinational logging corpora-tions to receive and profit from public property that was illegally sold by the government of British Columbia, and upheld by the courts of British Columbia. The entire tenure system of British Columbia is based on thievery and corruption.

"I understand, sir, that the courts of Canada, the courts of B.C., are supposed to be apolitical in nature, and the decisions made in court-rooms are expected to be uninfluenced by the political opinions of the people making the decisions. I find this expectation sort of silly, on the vain side, and contrary to all collective experience. Who among us can rise above our most deeply held convictions and be entirely objective?

"... We are all political here, sir, whether or not we call it by that name. And the main political belief of those who are in power in this country, in this province, is that the primary business of this country, this province, is business itself.

"I submit, sir, that a significant portion of the population is becom-ing uncomfortable with this notion. When people see large segments of our life-support systems disappearing, when the health and finan-cial costs of the chemicalization, computerization and robotization of industry become glaringly apparent, when the very reproductive processes, including those of humans, are taken over by greedy biotech corporations who try to patent the life process itself, then sig-nificant numbers of people start questioning the premise that the main purpose of life is business."

Am I getting boring? Probably. I tend to preach. Like Daddy. To get on a roll and not know when to stop. Which gives everybody a headache, especially my kids. Especially Marian. "Mom," she will say firmly, giving me a warning look. Then I know I am approaching her limit. And I'll back off. Unless we happen to be at a party or other gathering; then I am protected by outsiders and will ignore her warning signals and preach on until everybody has turned glassy-eyed or walked away.

Damn my Daddy! That's just the way he was. I've turned into my father. But I've got to get on with my address to the court. I have an opportunity here to really preach the gospel according to Betty ...

"... Sir, the famous French writer and philosopher Simone de Beauvoir wrote a book before she died about ageing in different cultures. In this book, entitled *Old Age*, Madame de Beauvoir points out that the human female is the only female in all of nature who lives for such a very long time after the reproductive cycle is finished. And Madame de Beauvoir came to what I think is a profound conclusion: that is, that somewhere along the line of evolution Mother Nature decided that grandmothers were good for the human species. And as nature's main concern is for species survival, Madame de Beauvoir's conclusion was that nature made a distinct decision that grandmothers were needed to ensure the survival of the species."

Let's hear it for grandmothers! Grandmothers arise! We have nothing to lose except our cookie sheets! But in all fairness, it isn't only grandmothers who must come forward, it's grandfathers, too. So I continue ...

"But the elders of both sexes in Western civilization have been elbowed out of our traditional roles as moderators of the society and stewards of the land. We have become disconnected from the young by the worship of technology, by the preoccupation with youth and the fear of ageing, by the demands and dictates of volatile and gyrating financial markets. We have become disconnected from the young by the internet, which is largely driven by pornography, where pedophiles are free to proclaim the use of children as sex objects, where young women, in efforts to meet suitable young men take foolhardy chances, where young men are taught to be violent to women, other men, and the earth itself through videos and film. We are separated from the young by the supreme corporate value that anything that sells is good, regardless of what it is, and finally we are separated from the young by what may prove to be the most profound separation of all ... by the fact that every five- and ten-dollar bill that comes into any Canadian or American hand holds traces of cocaine."

How could this have happened? Where are the protectors of society? Are there no adults left to protect the children? It's as though the entire world has become bereft of adults. Big, greedy, ignorant, violence-prone kids dressed up in suits and ties as well as battle gear— the suits and camouflage wearers are brothers under the skin—are greedy for wars, contracts, arms, computers, stock market deals. Winning is the only thing. This mentality is running our world, turning it around and around ...

But I can't stop for rumination, keep focused ...

"But elders are increasingly persuaded by all that is popular in the culture that these issues are really none of our business and that we couldn't do anything about the degradation of the earth and democracy if we tried. Better to just enjoy our retirement.

"Too many of our numbers, at least the ones who can afford it, are in the grip of what I call 'elder chic.' The more affluent ones cruise to the Bahamas or some lesser-known, more exotic resort; others play golf, enjoy their condos, their swimming pools; the less affluent ones are on their way to Las Vegas to play the slots on some kind of bargain flight, or off to Bingo. And nowhere are elders portrayed in society in their historical roles.

"The trivial choices dangled before the elders of Western society today are a rotten trade-off. Self-indulgent, peripheral pleasures are urged upon us while real life-affirming responsibility is denied. And the world suffers. Large segments of the world die every day from neglect and non-involvement by elders. And this has been the greatest coup d'état the corporate world has ever accomplished because when elders are divorced from the young in most meaningful ways, then the elders are cast aside and the young are cast adrift. And all corporations know very well, regardless of what they are selling, that insecure people buy more things. And when the more sensitive of our number get bogged down with all this stuff, this surfeit of shallowness, there are always the doctors who, driven by the drug companies, are only too happy to hand out highly addictive 'happy pills.'

"The Canadian Party of Women, of which I am a member, has a unique mindset concerning what remains of the public forests of British Columbia. We do not believe that any remaining old-growth public forests should be cut. We believe that all logging of public old-growth forests should stop. Now. Other people, and sometimes even our friends, try to tell us that this is an impossible dream, that we must think of the forest workers, too, there are jobs at stake here. In spite of my own union background and my working-class identification, my only response is this: care for the environment must supersede temporary jobs. If the only jobs this society, this economic system, this country, this province can provide are jobs that destroy the life-support systems of the earth, then the entire economic system should be dismantled and we should start over again from scratch and try to create a saner system.

"Sir, the reason I don't think I am a dreamer of impossible dreams is because I am a student of history. And if there is one thing that history has demonstrated over and over again it is that all power ultimately lies with the people, with the will and consent of the governed.

Laws change, shift, are modified along with the changing, shifting, modifying thinking of the body politic. These two entities are constantly interacting, colliding often, evolving in fits and starts, but as long as change is possible then the dance goes on."

There. That concludes part one of my address to Mr. Justice Parrett. Which, I am sure, will have very little impact. Nevertheless, it is my time to speak, and with that off my chest, I can concentrate on the second part, which will be purely the legalities of arrest and charge under an injunction as opposed to arrest under the Criminal Code. I am not a lawyer and have no legal training, and one could make the case that I am ill-equipped to argue points of law before the Supreme Court of British Columbia. However, for years I have been reading and thinking about these injunctions that are given out as a matter of course by the justices of the province. I may not be an expert on the subject, but I am well-versed in the matter, as it is a subject about which I feel passionately.

I retire that night reasonably satisfied. But there is something nagging at me about my mother, something unresolved, so that when my mind slips away from the immediate tasks at hand, it drifts back to that last summer of two years ago after Aunt Gladys fell, and the lives of the two elderly sisters hung in the balance.

Chapter Ten

The entire time that I was running to the hospital and back seeing about Aunt Gladys, the Mississippi sun was burning brighter and hotter by the day. No relief in sight. And underneath all of the frantic activity, I was worried about Andy. He was having more tests to determine what the cancer was doing. On the third afternoon of Aunt Gladys' rehospitalization, I heard Mama rattling pots and pans in the kitchen. It was only four-thirty, way too early for dinner.

"Mama, what are you doing?" I asked, going in.

"I thought we'd have an early supper so we can get to the hospital and back before dark."

Mama and Aunt Gladys both had a fear of being out on the road after dark with me at the wheel. I couldn't understand it. I had been hit several times but I'd never once done the hitting. I had a flawless driving record, but both sisters were convinced that I was a danger on the highway.

"Mama, you just saw Aunt Gladys this morning and the doctor said she needed to rest. We'll go again first thing in the morning. And it's too hot to think about cooking. We'll go out and eat in a bit, okay? Where would you like to go?"

Mama blinked at me for a moment and then put the skillet back in its place under the counter.

"Well, I don't rightly know," she said thoughtfully.

Ordinarily, this question would keep Mama and Aunt Gladys

occupied for at least an hour. After much discussion they would decide on a certain place to eat, undecide, then decide again. But Mama knew I didn't like this game, that in fact I refused to play it.

I refused to play their other favourite word game, too, the one about parking and locking the car. Parking anywhere, anytime, even back in their own driveway. Mama would say, "Oh, let's don't bother locking the car this time, this car is too old for anybody to steal," and Aunt Gladys would counter with, "But you know, Bug, they are stealing old cars these days," and then Mama would capitulate and say "Okay, let's lock it," at which point Aunt Gladys would become generous, too, and say, "Oh, let's not bother. If you think it's okay we'll just leave it." Mama and Aunt Gladys would lob this possibility back and forth indefinitely until I wanted to scream. Which I finally did one day, more or less, co-opting the discussion by issuing a decree that from that day forward the car would be locked every time we left it anywhere, for any reason, so there would be no need for further discussion on the matter. And they were both so put out with me that I finally had to acknowledge that this ongoing exchange was part of a ritual on which I had no right to intrude.

"Let's go to the casino to eat," Mama said with only a moment's consideration. "The one that fries such good catfish. I'm hungry for some fried catfish."

At ninety-five, Mama's digestion was remarkable. She could eat fried foods with gusto, along with the hottest of hot peppers. She had passed these two loves along to me. Anything good to eat was even better if it was fried and laced with hot peppers. I hated going to the casinos to eat, but if that's where Mama wanted to go, we would head out at six-thirty.

The Vicksburg waterfront is full of gambling riverboats. I've read reports that in the casinos of towns like Vicksburg most of the profits come from poor whites and even poorer blacks. Other local businesses suffer, too, as money that should be going for food, new clothing, better housing, all gets thrown to the slots and gaming tables. Poor people in general must figure the odds are so stacked against them that the only possible way out is to win some kind of a jackpot. I used to rant and rave to anyone who would listen that any society that promotes gambling is morally and spiritually bankrupt, but while Mama agreed with me in principle, she still liked to eat at the casinos and throw a few bucks at the slots while she was at it. I didn't know how she reconciled this with her religious beliefs. I didn't ask. I had enough of my own contradictions to deal with.

Anyone can walk into a casino and have a perfectly delicious meal for next to nothing. Oh, yes, the dens of iniquity are extremely seductive. A free pull at one of the big slots upstairs comes with every lunch or dinner bill. And then, of course, after the free pull, well, it couldn't hurt to try one or two more—after all, dinner was almost free. And so most people wind up paying a lot more for their dinner than if they had flown to New Orleans and eaten at Antoine's. Or dined in a posh restaurant in Paris, France, for that matter. I knew instinctively that the only way to beat the casinos was to refuse the first free slot ticket. But as I was there with Mama, I would most certainly partake of the dinner.

We sat next to the huge glass window that overlooked the river. Oh, it was so beautiful, the way the Mississippi, dotted with small craft, rolled sullenly but gracefully beneath us, past the riverboats, headed Gulfward. When I was a kid we could eat anything that came out of the river; now it was so polluted it wasn't even safe to look at. Multinational corporations and smaller companies began the toxic waste dumping high in its headwaters up north. By the time the poor river got to Vicksburg, it could hardly move under the burden of sludge and poisons it carried to the Gulf of Mexico. The crisp, tasty fried catfish Mama was eating probably came from a fish farm. Its conditions of origin? Only the Goddess knows.

I tackled the huge mound of shrimp on my own plate. I love the spicy, sweetly curled little pink things. I ignored the tables of Cajun cooking, the soul food, roast beef, chicken cooked three different ways, crayfish bisque, three different kinds of rice, hot biscuits, corn bread, fried okra, yams, fried oysters and crab legs and went straight to the shrimp. By the time we were ready to leave, the pile of shrimp shells on my plate was staggering.

"Betty, don't they have shrimp in Canada?" Mama asked as we were leaving the dining room. I laughed and said no, certainly not in the quantities one found in Louisiana and Mississippi restaurants. I noticed that Mama held my arm for support more firmly than usual as we took the escalator upstairs for her turn with the free slot tickets, her turn and mine. While she was being lulled by the machine, I felt the wad of shrimp in my belly take an uneasy turn. The shrimp were trying to swim around in the half gallon of iced tea I had washed them down with. And a headache was toying with the left side of my brain. I didn't get headaches often, but when I did, they were killers. By the time Mama had given up dreams of instant riches and I was helping her into the car in the casino parking lot, the headache had ceased its toying and had established a firm beachhead. But I noticed that Mama winced when I buckled her up.

"What's the matter?" I asked.

"Nothing. I'm just full as a tick. All that catfish. Let's get home."

I pulled out of the casino lot that led to the main highway, but even before we reached the turn off to the old country road that would take us home I suspected there might be trouble. I didn't feel well and Mama didn't look too well, either. And the car's air conditioning unit was signalling that it wasn't great, either, in spite of the recent repairs. But we were in traffic and there was no way to go but forward. My head was splitting and the shrimp inside my belly just wanted out. Finally, finally, just as we approached the familiar turn off that would gently lead us home, Mama nudged me.

"Betty, that's a police car behind us. I think he's motioning us to pull over."

"Fuck," I said, in absolute total frustration. The word I had never used before in my mother's hearing, the word my sons never said in front of me, the word my daughters and I quarrelled over when they used it, or tried to, the mother of all cuss words in the English language, the word, the word, oh, yes, the word. Fuck. There. Mama's reaction was immediate. And furious.

"Girl, you want me to slap you upside the head? You watch your mouth. And pull over like the cop is telling you to."

I pulled over. And laughed. It's a nervous habit. Whenever I am overwhelmed with the struggle of life, when events seem to just spin out of hope of any kind of control, I laugh. But the officer who walked over to our car and ordered me to step out wasn't laughing. And he certainly didn't laugh when I obeyed his instructions, stepped out of the car, and as if on some kind of cosmic cue, promptly vomited all over his shiny black shoes.

"My God, woman, look what you did to my shoes!" the officer exclaimed as he jumped backward out of the mess of only partially digested shrimp and red spicy cocktail sauce.

I was too ill to reply. My stomach was heaving again and I held onto the side of the car door for support. A second officer suddenly appeared beside the first. He looked at the shrimp mess on his buddy's shoes and then at me.

"You been weaving on the road, ma'am. You been drinking?" he asked politely but firmly.

I shook my head. Which was a mistake. The officers swayed before my stricken eyes.

"You leave my daughter alone!" Mama yelled loudly from inside the car. "She don't drink. She ain't had nothing to drink. She just ate too many doggone shrimp. She lives in Canada. They don't have shrimp in Canada."

The second officer sidestepped the shrimp mess on the ground and peered past me into the car. He was older than the first officer, and much heavier. Not that I could see all that well by now, even up close. The migraine had captured the entire front left lobe of my brain and was trying to cut off my vision.

"Hey there, ma'am," the officer said pleasantly to my mother. "I think I know you, ma'am. And I think I know this car. Ain't you Gladys' sister?"

"Yes, sir, I surely am," Mama answered. "Who are you?"

"Lewis Largilo. I met you at Don Roy's funeral. Do you recollect?"

"Well, you surely look familiar."

"Yes, ma'am. I've known Gladys for thirty-five, almost forty years. I first met her when she was running that little restaurant out by the university. How she doing?"

"Not too good, Lewis. She's in the hospital right now. That's where Betty's been all day, seeing about Gladys. Gladys fell and broke a rib and jarred her hip and Betty's been so busy looking after Gladys she didn't get nothing to eat all day until we went to the casino and then she ate a barrel of shrimp and it made her sick ..."

Officer Lewis turned back to me.

"You do look poorly, ma'am. Do you want to see a doctor?"

The man was no longer a threat. He was almost kin.

"No, it's a headache," I explained. "A migraine. Once I get home I'll be fine."

"Well, I can't let you drive there, ma'am. Not in your condition. You all staying with Miss Gladys out at the mobile home park?"

"Yes."

Officer Lewis nodded. He would drive our car, he said, and his buddy would follow behind in the police car. He kept up a pleasant chatter as he helped Mama into the back seat, me into the front passenger seat. I didn't have to do anything but sit there, which was all right with me. Every movement jarred my head. After fastening his seat belt around his own substantial bulk, he drove us down the turn off road.

"If you have to throw up some more, just holler and I'll pull over," he said kindly. I turned and looked at him with the good side of my head. He was actually rather handsome, with wavy salt-and-pepper hair and warm brown eyes.

"I'm glad I came along," he went on, smiling over at me.

"Thank you, sir," I managed. "You're very kind."

"Why, not a bit. No siree. I'm happy to do something for Miss Gladys' folks. She helped me a whole lot my first year in university. If it hadn't been for her and her little restaurant I'd have plumb starved to death. I was living on six dollars a week. Just think of that! When I ran slap out of money I'd go to your auntie and she'd give me a little something to do around the place and then feed me and I'd leave with a bag of leftovers to take back to my room. She's a mighty fine woman, your Aunt Gladys."

Christ, this was making me feel even sicker.

"Yes, a mighty fine woman, your auntie," he reiterated. "She was good to me."

Yeah, and I bet she seduced you in the bargain, I thought, but of course I didn't say it. I was in no position to be sarcastic to Officer Lewis. We were soon home and the neighbours were at their front doors and windows to witness the spectacle, especially the ones with religious signs on their lawns predicting the end of the world. Oh yes, they strained to see who was driving Miss Gladys' car—why, it was a police officer, and for heaven's sake there's a regular police car behind them, and just look, Miss Gladys' niece can hardly walk, she and her Mama both have to be helped in by police officers, they must both be drunk. Whoever would have thought it, why, we didn't know Miss Bug drank at all, but who can tell about her daughter, she moved to Canada, you know, why would a body from the South want to do that, and she don't go to church, you know …

Once inside, Mama called Geraldine, Sonny's wife, to come over. The officers, satisfied they had done their duty to friends and citizenry, left. Geraldine rushed over, bearing an ice pack for me, and eager for the details of our escapade. I was left blissfully alone in the coolness of Aunt Gladys' bedroom while Mama explained to Geraldine in the next room how we wound up with police officers escorting us home. I could hear Mama's voice clearly over the hum of the air conditioner.

"Good thing it turned out to be a fellow who knew Gladys," Mama said. "You know how Betty drives. You're always on the verge of seeing your maker right close up when you get into a car with her, even when she's feeling good ..."

Oh, God. The pounding in my head. My head could fly off my neck altogether and I wouldn't even care. But maybe if I didn't move at all, I thought, not even a hair. The last migraine I had was in the palliative care unit almost three years ago when Dr. Gabor Maté told me that I should tell Barbara Ellen that it was okay for her to die.

"She wants your permission to die," he said gently. We were in a private room reserved especially for people like me. The most wretched people on earth.

"To hell with that!" I flung at him, shocked and horrified at the very suggestion. "She doesn't have my permission to die! I forbid it ..."

I broke down at that point and sobbed wildly. The doctor waited patiently. He was used to this reaction. This was his job.

"Mrs. Krawczyk, I think you do understand that Barbara Ellen's suffering will simply increase now, by the hour ..."

"She's not suffering! She has the butterfly in her arm. She talked to her sisters and her father this morning, she saw friends just yesterday, she was talking to her little boy, and hugging him ..."

"That was a gift. A gift she gave loved ones. To tell everybody goodbye. You're the only one she hasn't told goodbye. She wants to do this now. She wants your permission to leave ..."

"Oh, please, don't! Who do you think you are, God? How do you know the hour of her death?"

And then I was reduced to begging. "Give me a few more days, please. Please put the IV back in ..."

"She doesn't want it. You have to be strong enough to give your daughter what she needs right now. She needs you to help her, to let her go; that's the only way you can help her now, to let her go …"

"God, how I hate this life. I can't bear it …"

"Yes, you can. Your family depends on you. Barbara is depending on you," Dr. Maté said.

That headache was so bad I thought I might expire before Barbara Ellen did. But I didn't. By the following evening I had recuperated enough to tell my daughter that if she was tired of being sick and wanted to go, I would no longer try to keep her. She held my hand and told me she would wait for me wherever it was she was going, and she died that morning, in my arms, her sister Marian holding her, too, her father also by her side. I wept silently into Aunt Gladys' blue satin pillow, remembering.

Mama tiptoed in with an ice pack. The room was dark and cool. I caught Mama's hand as she positioned the ice pack against my forehead and pressed it against my cheek. She had large, capable hands with long fingers, fingers that were rarely still, fingers that could even then race up and down the keyboard of a piano or accordion with joy and exuberance, or coax a swath of material into a fetching child's garment, concoct wonderful things to eat, or grasp a hoe handle with a decisive grip. Her fingers felt cool to my flushed cheek.

"I love you," I whispered.

"I love you, too. Go to sleep now."

I didn't wake until ten o'clock the next morning. Mama was nudging my shoulder.

"Andy is on the phone," she said. "Do you want me to tell him to call back?"

I sat up. The blinding force of the headache had retreated. There was only a dull throbbing in my left temple. And Mama was dressed to go out. Of course. Aunt Gladys. We must get to the hospital.

"Why didn't you wake me sooner?" I asked, noting the late hour on Aunt Gladys' cute kitten clock.

"Because you needed to rest. Geraldine is waiting in her car to take me to see Gladys. After you talk to Andy, go back to bed."

"Yes ma'am," I said. Satisfied, Mama left.

I picked up the bedside phone with stiff fingers. Andy? Had the tests returned already? Would he know now?

"Hello, Mother," he said.

"Andy ..."

"It's good, Mother. The tests were good. The tumour has all but disappeared. They had trouble finding it. I'm on the mend."

Relief flooded my body. I felt light-headed, giddy even.

"Oh, Andy, that's so wonderful! Tell me everything. I want to hear everything."

He told me the doctors were puzzled at the way the tumour was behaving. Andy's cancer was rare; the doctors did not know much about it. The chemotherapy mix they had brewed was a wild shot in the dark, but it was working—it was working far better than the doctors themselves could have imagined. Andy wasn't going to follow Barbara into the Great Divide, not yet, not yet, he was a fighter ...

I called the other kids, my heart lighter than it had been in days, months, since Andy was first diagnosed a year ago. At the time I was almost overwhelmed with the ghastly news that another of my eight children had been stricken and was in mortal danger. How in God's name could that happen? My children were young and healthy; there was some cancer in the family, yes, but the family was so large it was almost impossible, given the statistics, for there not to be. But now I am the bearer of good news. Andy is radically improved.

There was a collective sigh of relief from Andy's siblings as I talked to them or left messages. Just as I hung up from talking to Rose Mary, Marian called. I filled her in on Andy's latest results.

"Oh, Mom, that's just so great. How wonderful! I know how worried you've been, how worried everybody has been. And I know Angie's relieved. My God, they've been through hell. I guess a marriage either collapses entirely or grows stronger under such a strain."

"Yes. Which reminds me. How are you getting on with your pharmacist?"

The pharmacist was Marian's latest interest, but my question evoked only a big sigh. Marian was twenty-eight at the time and had been officially engaged once to a Canadian professor and semi-engaged later to a young man from Mississippi who followed her back to Canada. In both instances, because of Marian's sudden panic attacks, unexplained rashes and full-blown hypochondria as the wedding dates approached, the weddings had been first postponed and then cancelled. Marian was not ready to be married at those times in her life. But she was definitely into romance.

"Oh, Mom, you don't want to know."

"Yes, I do. Geraldine took Mama to the hospital to see Aunt Gladys so I have time. Weren't you going away with him for the weekend?"

"Yes, we went. But you remember I told you there seemed to be a bit of dysfunction in the sex department?"

"You, uh ... indicated that. Maybe you better talk to your sisters or your friends about this."

"Oh, don't cop out on me, Mom. We're just talking sex now, not relationships. Anyway, we did go away on the weekend and absolutely nothing happened."

"Well, where did you go?"

"To his cabin by the lake. It was quiet and peaceful and beautiful. And not a damn thing happened. We've been seeing each other for four months and nothing has ever happened. We make out a little and that's it."

"Is it a religious or philosophic thing with him?"

"No."

"Well, let's see ... has Viagra crept into your conversations?"

"No."

"Well, is the man dead?" I asked.

"No, he isn't dead," she answered, her voice taking on a sardonic edge. "If he were, I might be able to work with a cadaver, you know, a little rigor mortis ..."

"Marian!" I yelled into the phone. Sometimes my children do succeed in shocking me. Which delights them.

"All right," Marian said, her voice full of barely suppressed laughter. "It just goes to show what a pitiful state I'm in that I have to call my mother down in Mississippi to tell her about my lack of anything remotely resembling a love life."

"It's okay, honey. That man wouldn't have been good for you, anyway. He's a capitalist."

She giggled. "Right. And I told him what you said about him having to undergo a purging ritual of some sort for owning all that real estate before he could be introduced to the family."

"Which probably didn't help his sexual dysfunction any," I answered.

"Well, I'm not going to worry about it. I don't have time. I'm just going to throw this one back; he's too weird."

Marian hung up and I wandered into the kitchen in search of juice and Tylenol. After that I showered and dressed. My stomach was still too queasy to eat, but at least the juice and Tylenol stayed down. Armed with more apple juice, I went out to the front porch and settled down in front of the fans. After a while I noticed that Sweetie had sought the comfort of the porch fans, too, and was watching me with a wary expression from her perch on the little redwood table.

"Oh, don't give me that look," I admonished her. "I'm not going to bother you. You think you're all I've got to worry about? You flatter yourself, you spoiled brat of a cat."

She hunkered down, ears flattened, eyes narrowed. And then a wave of pity for her washed over me. Whenever Aunt Gladys was in the hospital, Sweetie was at loose ends. She was afraid, with her feline intuition, that Aunt Gladys might not return. Would she then be left in my care, she probably wondered? The notion made me laugh. Sweetie gave a start and scuttled off the porch into the yard and under Ray Allen's mobile.

"Good riddance, you silly thing," I flung after her, but without malice. I propped my bare feet up on Mama's patio ottoman and tried to think. I should call my brother.

Ray Allen and Carol had just spent a two-month sojourn with Mama and Aunt Gladys shortly before I came. Having paid their dues they had headed for the hills, where they have a small acreage with a summer mobile home in the Mongolian Rim in northern Arizona to ride out the worst of the summer heat. I would call after dinner, just to keep them informed. And my nephew Jean, over in Baton Rouge. I should alert him to have Mama's apartment ready, just in case.

I like my sister's kids. I just can't relate to them. They all belong to either a fundamentalist Catholic movement within the church or some kind of fundamentalist Protestant charismatic church. Fundamentalists, all. Male godhead worshipers, all. Thinking about it, I felt a surge of annoyance at my dead sister. Oh, Doris, why did you have to plant this religion thing between us so that your children and mine are strangers and aliens to each other? Wasn't Mama's and Daddy's religion enough for the entire line, for Pete's sake? Why couldn't you and I have been real friends and confidants instead of diffident distant relations with only an occasional emotional connection? Why couldn't you understand that your drinking and pill-taking was a health problem and not a religious sin? Guilt, guilt, it dragged us all down.

The phone rang. What utter luxury to have a porch phone. Ray Allen had installed it so Mama and Aunt Gladys wouldn't break a leg trying to answer the one in the kitchen. It was Margaret Elizabeth, answering my message. I related the details of Andy's tests and brought her up to date on Aunt Gladys' state of being.

"So things are looking good, Mom," she said. "When are you coming home?"

"I'm not sure, honey. I may have to stay another month." And then, remembering she had mentioned a trip to Victoria with her husband, Andre, I asked about that.

"It was good. Sort of."

"What does that mean?" I inquired.

"We stayed with Sam and Penny. And they're just the perfect couple. They're so polite and affectionate with each other all the time. I mean, all the time."

"So?" I asked.

"So it cramps my style. It's like Rose Mary said about her kids and company. Sometimes it's a strain making the kids mind with other people around, and as soon as the company leaves she starts yelling, 'Have you kids gone mad, stop doing that this instant, go to your rooms, you're grounded, both of you, all of you, and no dessert!'—you know, the way she usually carries on with them when they're hyped up. I feel much the same with Andre. I can't chastise him the way I usually do when other people are around, so it's a relief to get home where I can abuse him in my normal fashion."

I laughed. Andre is tall and muscular and athletic. Margaret is small-boned and slender.

"Don't make me laugh," I protested. "I've still got the residue of a headache."

"Don't be away too long, Mom. We saw Julian over the weekend. He misses you."

Mention of Julian tugged at my heart. Separation anxiety. He was only seven years old; I had a right to feel anxious. The little boy Barbara had left behind lived with his father in Victoria. His father was devoted, but Julian also needed a grandmother's firm hand. I told Margaret goodbye and hung up. Immediately, the phone rang again. I picked it up eagerly, expecting to hear from Mike, my middle son, in answer to my message. But it wasn't Mike. It was the hospital. Gladys, I thought. She must have taken a turn for the worse. But no. The woman on the phone wasn't talking about Aunt Gladys. She was talking about Mama. Mama has had a heart attack! I must come at once.

Chapter Eleven

Mama, oh, Mama, please be okay, don't die on me just yet, I'm not ready for you to go, my heart was begging as I burst into emergency.

"My mother," I gasped to the woman at the desk. "Winifred Shiver. She's had a heart attack."

"Oh, yes. You're her daughter?"

"Yes. Where is she?"

"They've just taken her upstairs to room 302."

"Is she …?"

"The doctor is with her. She's waiting for you."

I hurried to the elevators, somewhat relieved but unsure what to think. If Mama was being put in a regular room instead of intensive care, had she really had a heart attack?

"It's a blockage," Dr. Hartrix explained to me outside Mama's hospital room.

"What does that mean?" I asked impatiently. I always try to give women the benefit of the doubt simply because we have to make do in a man's world, but I didn't like Dr. Hartrix. A woman of more than ample proportions, she had a soft, insinuating voice that got on my nerves. Because in spite of her soft, nicey-nice voice, she had absorbed all of the patronizing male arrogance that the medical establishment had to offer.

"One of the main arteries leading to her heart has been partially closed by a blockage. I've given her something for pain. She's resting comfortably right now."

"But what does this mean? Is she going to die? Right away?"

"It's hard to tell. But I think I would go ahead and inform the other relatives."

I stared at her, trying to digest this sudden information.

"But isn't there something you can do for my mother besides painkillers?" I blurted. She gave me a small, patient smile.

"Mrs. ..."

"Krawczyk," I snapped. The woman could never remember my name. It was a difficult name and usually I didn't care—the name wasn't mine anyway, it was Wally's name—but I hadn't jettisoned the thing and now I was known by that name.

"Isn't there anything else you can do for my mother?" I asked, giving my voice permission to become louder and broader.

"Mrs. Krawczyk, your mother is ninety-five years old."

"So? What does that mean? That you're not going to do anything to help her because she's ninety-five years old?"

A deep sigh escaped Dr. Hartrix's pursed lips. That sigh said oh, it's just so difficult to deal with ignorant, emotional relatives ...

"I want a cardiologist to see her," I said firmly.

Dr. Hartrix shifted gears slightly. "Well, of course you have a right to call in a cardiologist, but the most he would do is order a blood thinner ..."

"Then that's what I want for my mother. Right now. Until the cardiologist can see her."

Another sigh. Deeper this time. "If you insist."

My eyes bored deep into hers. I wanted to strangle her. On the spot.

"I insist," I said. "I really do insist. I want my mother to have the same care your children would want for you were you in my mother's position." And if you don't give it to her I will sue you, I added silently.

Dr. Hartrix picked up on my silent message. "Very well. We'll have to take her down to intensive care."

"Good. Take her down."

Dr. Hartrix turned away, walked quickly over to the nurses' station and began ordering Mama's transfer. Good. We understood each other. I went into Mama's room. It would be different, I told myself, if Mama weren't basically so healthy. She could make a hundred if that poor excuse of a doctor would get off her hefty haunches and stop playing God with my one and only mother.

It didn't take long for the stretcher brigade to appear, and Mama was wheeled out of the room and down the hall. I trotted along beside the wheeled stretcher.

"Just because I got a little pain in my shoulder," Mama complained at the indignity of being wheeled about. "And a tad lightheaded when I was talking to Gladys. Now they're treating me like I'm crippled. I want to go home. Me and Gladys can't both be up here at the same time."

"And why not?" I asked as we all stopped for the service elevator. "Actually, I'm thinking about checking in myself. The food's not really that bad. In fact, I've heard that office workers come from all over town to eat here in the cafeteria because the food's so good."

"That ain't possible," Mama answered dryly as the elevator opened to admit us. Down in the dungeons Mama was settled into one of the intensive care rooms. It was hardly bigger than a cubicle, with one entire wall lined with machinery and electronics. A young male Filipino nurse came in and started hooking Mama up to the wires and tubes. He asked her a few questions as he worked, but she couldn't seem to understand him.

"Your mother has trouble with my accent," he said apologetically when he had finished. "I'm sorry."

"It's all right," I answered. "When she recovers from the shock that one of the nurses in this unit is a man, she'll set her mind more on what you're actually saying."

He flashed me a white smile and left.

"I don't want a man for a nurse," Mama said as soon as he had gone.

"Why not? You've had men doctors."

"That's different. Men are supposed to be doctors."

"But you have a woman doctor."

"I just inherited her. She's Gladys' doctor. It's just easier for both of us to go to the same doctor. I'm not crazy about her, either. But did she tell you how long I have to be here?"

"No," I said. "But she'll talk to us later. Close your eyes and get some rest."

"Stop bossing me," she answered. "And just remember who's the mama."

But her words were becoming slurred. The pain medicine was taking effect. She closed her eyes and was soon fast asleep. It wasn't long before Dr. Hartrix tiptoed in to check Mama's machines. She whispered that a cardiologist would be in to see Mama in an hour or so. The she left, two deep, disapproving lines on each of her flushed cheeks.

And to hell with you, I flung silently after her. The woman lying in this bed is a better woman than you'll probably ever be and she is most certainly worthy of her breath. I sat down in the chair by

156

Mama's bed. Her glasses were on the bedside table. I folded them carefully and leaned over to place them in the nightstand drawer. Momentarily I was overcome by a wave of dizziness. It reminded me that I hadn't eaten since expelling the shrimp the day before.

•

That last summer two years ago with my mother and Aunt Gladys both in the hospital fades before my eyes in the buffet room on the ferryboat, where I'm eating shrimp again. I'm on my way from Vancouver to Victoria to apartment-sit for my friend Marian Stoodley in Victoria, and hopefully to spend some time with my grandson Julian. I love the hour-and-a-half ferry ride between the two cities. The buffet room on the sixth deck has glass windows all the way around so you can watch the islands pass by as you eat. Sunrises and sunsets in good weather can be stupendous, and the food in the buffet room is adequate, if not delectable. Compared to prison fare, it is a feast. Night has fallen by the time I arrive at my friend's apartment, and she and the cat are waiting for me. The cat is named Cairo. It's a kitten, really.

Shortly after arriving, I call Julian's father. I learn I can't have Julian the following day; however, I may have him for most of the rest of the week. Satisfied with that, I make tentative plans to visit my other grandchildren up-island for the following week. And then by the time I get back, Mr. Justice Parrett's decision on my guilt or innocence will be ready.

I have asked Mr. Justice Parrett to throw out my case entirely. I told him in the second part of my address to the court that I was not arguing that I shouldn't be held responsible for my actions, but that I had been deprived of my rights under the Charter by being charged with contempt of court rather than for blocking a road. I quoted other judges who have come out recently supporting this point of view, that all anti-logging protesters should be charged, like everyone else, under the Criminal Code. But I feel sure Mr. Justice Parrett isn't one of the justices leaning in this direction, although I first heard about the article in the UBC *Law Review* concerning the writ of Mandamus from him. Under this law, if the RCMP are not doing their duty by arresting someone in the act of a crime, they can be made to arrest them when someone asks the court to issue a writ of Mandamus. My stance is that the RCMP should have arrested me for blocking a road instead of waiting for three days until Interfor decided they wanted to have me arrested under an injunction.

Before I left Vancouver I composed my address to the judge on sentencing. In fact, I have brought a copy with me to show my friend Marian. But we don't get around to it. By the time we catch up on gossip and get to bed, it's late. At daybreak she leaves in a flurry, still dispensing last-minute instructions as she carries out bags and parcels. The kitten and I play, have breakfast, play some more. Then Cairo disappears under the bed for his morning nap. I am left on my own. What I think I will do, I say aloud, is call the Friends of the Elaho.

I get Shari Mustafia on the phone. Shari is the young woman who was beaten by the Interfor loggers and their friends on September 15, 1999, and was hospitalized. She gives me astounding news. Seventeen people were arrested yesterday in the Elaho. One was charged with mischief and sixteen others were charged with aiding and abetting mischief. People were being arrested on the flimsiest of charges to discourage others from even being in the area to witness the carnage among the old growth. And if that wasn't bad enough, the day before, which was August 30, 2000, not quite a year after the raid on the camp in the Elaho Valley, two other people were kicked and punched to the ground by Interfor employees in Bella Coola. I hang up, stunned.

But what to do? I've already blockaded in the Elaho twice. And I must visit with my grandson. Plus here I am in charge of this kitten. What I would really like to do is simply talk to the Premier. I would like to know what he actually knows about the violence Interfor employees and their associates are using against citizens who are worried about our forests. I have tried to talk to the Premier before without success, but this is such an urgent matter I must try again.

I spend the rest of the afternoon contacting friends in Victoria, telling them of my outrage at what has happened and that I have decided to pitch a tent on the lawn of the legislature and refuse to leave until the Premier agrees to talk to me. I want to impress on him the need for a moratorium in the Elaho until the various claims by First Nations people, and environmentalists lobbying for a national park and citizens' claims of stewardship, can be sorted out. Without a moratorium, Interfor will simply gut the oldest, most valuable trees, while allowing their employees to use physical violence against protesters. Yes, I must talk to the Premier.

My friends rise to the challenge. Julian finds it all extremely interesting, the sign-making, the creation of pamphlets, the gathering of supplies for a tent-in, the cool young people involved. The Raging Grannies are contacted, speakers are scrounged up, the media are alerted. The event is planned for Wednesday, September sixth. Young David Ball is my right-hand man in the event, along with Shane Calder.

The first day the tent-in dawns bright and beautiful. When we arrive at the legislature lawn, it's all looking good. The Raging

Grannies sing. They're a group of older women who dress up in old-fashioned ruffles and hats a mile wide topped with gaudy artificial flowers, but there is nothing cutesy about the songs they sing. Their lyrics challenge the takeover of the world by corporations and military might. Everybody in the crowd loves them. Fifty or so people have gathered. It's an adequate turnout for a Wednesday lunch-hour gathering.

I had asked Shari Mustafia and Bryce Gilroy Scott to come over from Vancouver to speak. (Bryce was also beaten in the attack at the Elaho camp.) They talk about the violence, update us on the logging, and then I speak. The topic of Tree Farm Licenses and the way they are given out and protected by all the forces of law and order and government is very complex. My job as a granny is to make it as simple as possible, so I simplify, simplify, simplify. It eventually comes down to one or two basic points. Public forests in British Columbia belong to all the people of B.C. Interfor is a leasee of our land. If we don't like the leasee—a corporation masquerading as a person under the legal definition—then we can throw the rascals out. I am here to inform the Premier that according to a recent poll the majority of people will join me in my demand that the rascals be thrown out.

Who will come with me to inform the Premier that we mightily desire an audience? Some of the Raging Grannies, that's who. (I'm a Raging Granny myself, having been adopted by at least one chapter.) A dozen or more other people join us, and several legislative guards accompany us; they have to be on hand in any kind of a protest situation. But the door to the Premier's office is, of course, locked. I send a message with one of the guards that unless the Premier agrees to talk to me very soon, I will pitch a tent on the front lawn of the legislature until he does agree. The guard goes away. We wait fifteen minutes, just milling about. No reply from the Premier, who is in a meeting. Okay, up with the tent.

The signs go up, too. The signs are wonderful, especially the one David made: *State of emergency in the Elaho! Interfor's violence! Premier's silence!* Others call for protection for the earth, for new regulations in the forests, for a stop to the rampant destruction of our heritage, for peace, for justice ...

And we have lots of handouts. People stop by, talk, bring food, coffee. I am comforted by old friends who live in Victoria, people I've known for some time, and I meet lots of new friends. There is talk of other tents joining mine. We could have a sea of tents! But I know this isn't likely. The Premier can't allow me just to stay here. It is only a matter of time before I'm arrested. But I can't allow Interfor's violence to stand. How I despise their bully mentality!

And yet I do understand the concerns and even the desperation of the men who work in the forests. They have bought into the American-Canadian dream that what one owns, what one earns, signifies a man's worth. They want their kids to have good things, to be thought well of, to get a good education. Work, that's the answer to getting ahead. Haven't I been there, done that? It takes a radical re-evaluation of the entire universe as one knows it, to grasp the notion that the opposite is actually true: that less is better.

But it's when union loggers start ranting about how rotten protesters are for using civil disobedience that I part company with them. Because when loggers and other forest workers say disparaging things about civil disobedience, I am ashamed of belonging to the working class. These remarks show that the workers have no understanding or even passing knowledge of the history of their own unions. If it hadn't been for the Wobblies (Industrial Workers of the

World), there wouldn't even be unions on this continent. It was the Wobblies who gained for all of us the right to organize, and this basic right was won on the backs, on the flesh and blood, of men and women who knew firsthand the necessity of using civil disobedience. And a number of them paid for their determination with their lives.

I personally think the International Woodworkers of America (IWA, now known as the Industrial, Wood and Allied Workers) is a disgrace to these early men and women, who not only wanted better working conditions and more pay, they wanted a better world for everybody. They had a shared vision. They dreamed of a world where the forces of the people's will equalled the forces of the corporations' power; where human development was as important as economic progress. The only vision the IWA has is to collude with Interfor in plundering and devouring the last of the old growth in public forests. Their vision, like Interfor's, is the bottom line.

The IWA didn't fight for the workers' jobs when mechanization came into the woods. The IWA didn't resist the grapple yarders or the feller bunchers or other machines that sucked up union jobs. The IWA didn't protest the automation of the mills, which cost many more jobs. The IWA couldn't bow low enough in the dirt before all of the international logging companies, in their claim that we had to do these things to remain competitive.

And what the IWA accepted without question was the notion that the loss of jobs was primarily the fault of environmentalists, even when evidence to the contrary was right before their eyes. It is glaringly apparent that international logging companies simply cut and run in this province, leaving behind not only communities that are devastated by the loss of forestry jobs but whole mountains and valleys that are repulsive to tourists because they are stripped of life.

And that is the future of every rural community that thinks it's okay to destroy the very treasures that make them unique. I am not surprised when Interfor proves itself to be without mind except for money; it does bother me a great deal when the very people who should be in the forefront of this battle—the workers—align themselves with their bosses, accepting the notion that their values and goals and fortunes are the same.

But there are no IWA workers out this afternoon on the Parliament lawns, at least none who want to talk to me. The guards are keeping an eye on things, but so far nobody has made a move to arrest me. They will wait until later, I am told by veterans who have been through similar arrests. They will wait until there are no reporters around, and not many people.

In the meantime, a rousing contingent of protesters proclaiming the virtues of marijuana have come around the corner. There are approximately fifty of them. They sit on the legislature steps and their leader gives a speech. Then they all cheer and light up. David goes over and talks to the leader of the group, and the leader comes to my tent asking if I will address the group. Well, I never pass up a chance to address a group.

I walk over to the people sitting on the steps. They are mostly young, flower children and straight-looking types. I start off by telling them that, in my opinion, the government's insistence on linking marijuana with heroin and cocaine is a big mistake because the main effect of this is to weaken young people's faith in government altogether. Young people can see, because they aren't blind, that it is alcohol and tobacco that kill and maim people and ruin their lives. How many people have died from smoking marijuana? How many have been driven violently crazy and have committed rape, murder or mayhem while high on marijuana? Marijuana has the opposite effect. Marijuana mellows instead of activating antisocial impulses. And yet our prisons are overflowing with people who have been arrested on marijuana charges, while the government itself pushes alcohol and tobacco. In my opinion, this contradiction is one of the main reasons why young people are so alienated from government that most don't even bother to vote. Why bother to vote for those who make or go along with such mad, unreasonable and downright stupid decisions about substances that are rife in our society?

Well, the Premier may not want to talk to me, but I'm a big hit with the marijuana group. But more people are gathering around my tent. I spend the afternoon talking, talking, talking, having my picture taken around the tent and signs, hugging people, exchanging good wishes, and then around four-thirty people start to leave. At six, Nina Leach, my good friend and only pubic supporter back when I was a pariah in Ucluelet, leaves, promising to return later with hot soup. So do some of the other women, women who were affiliated with me in the Canadian Party of Women in Victoria. Shane stays with me. He will roll up in a bedroll under a tarp for the night if I am not arrested before nightfall, he says, just to make sure there is a witness to whatever happens. Some of the others have promised to return with tents, too. Dusk is gathering. A man from out of province stops by, wants to know the particulars of the protest. While I am talking to him, two guards come over.

"Ma'am, we're asking you to take down your tent," one of the guards says. He's a nice older man; I have spoken to him before.

"I'm waiting to see the Premier," I reply, stalling for time. Damn, the TV reporter just left. The guards were probably waiting for that. No reporters around now, only a handful of people.

"The Premier won't be coming to speak to you and there's a law against camping on the legislative lawn. I'm asking you to remove the tent and your belongings from this lawn. Will you comply?"

"Give me a few minutes to think about this," I say. The guards agree and walk away.

The others gather around me.

"David ... where the hell is the TV man?" I ask frantically

"I'm trying to get him right now," David answers, cellphone to his ear. "He left his number in case anything started to happen ..."

Which of course meant an arrest. TV people are primarily interested in action. Something dramatic. Conflict. Jerry Mander brought this home to me more than twenty years ago. In his book *Four Arguments for the Elimination of Television*, he pointed out that the way the little dots on the screen are positioned makes the screen ideally suited for portrayals of gross actions, and ill-suited for subtle ones. So violence, mayhem, floods, wars, devastation, any kind of physical conflict, these are great for television. But in spite of my issues with television, I have to try to stave off arrest until David can find the TV man. It's important that the people of British Columbia see what actually happens when a citizen who is protesting the decimation of public forests demands to talk to the Premier about it. I most decidedly want it on film. And David finally announces triumphantly that the TV man is on his way.

The guards are coming back now with the police, but the man from out of province turns out to be a lawyer. He engages the officers in conversation until one of the officers asks me point blank if this gentleman is representing me. I say, "Well, now, I'm not sure," and the gentleman says he can't represent me because he's from out of province. The officer announces that if I do not agree to pack up my tent and belongings I will be arrested. I see the TV man hurrying across the lawn, his camera at the ready, and there is no need to stall any longer. I tell the officer that I am not moving my tent because Chief Justice of Canada Beverley McLachlin said recently in an interview that Canadian law not only belongs to the lawmakers and the justices but it also belongs to the people, and this is my legislature and my lawn and I want to speak to the Premier ...

There are now four police officers surrounding me. I sink down to the ground and sit with my legs crossed. I have my little purse strapped to my back and a real backpack at the ready. I know what correctional centres are like now. Once inside, it takes a dozen written requests before one may or may not receive what was requested. I'm equipped with paper, pens, court papers, a dictionary and a thesaurus. There will be a half dozen different versions of the Bible stacked end on end in Maximum Security, but there will not be a dictionary or thesaurus in the entire unit. And one must buy one's own pens and paper and envelopes from the prison canteen. I don't know what people who are taken in with no money and no writing supplies do when they need to write a letter. I, for one, will go in prepared to keep a journal and write many letters. But before I get to the Burnaby Correctional Centre for Women, I must go through the indignity of being arrested.

There are four officers. I have two arms and two legs. The officers and my extremities are matched up and I am bodily lifted from the ground. The police wagon is parked by the side and to the rear of the main Parliament building. My supporters follow part of the way and I shout slogans from my upside-down position. The stars are beautiful. Finally we arrive at the police wagon and I am asked to cooperate and get inside. I say, "No, you must put me inside because I don't resist arrest but neither do I make it easy for arresting officers, as I am being separated from public property, my public property, and I don't agree to this." The officers hoist me in and lock the doors. I sit up in the wagon and examine my arms and legs. The arrest is over and I am unhurt. I relax against the back of the cab. This was the hard part. The rest will be easier. Or so I think.

Chapter Twelve

After I'm booked in at the jail, everything is taken away from me, including my court papers and documents. I find it shocking that I will be representing myself in court in the morning yet the very papers I need to defend myself are kept from me: a copy of the Charter of Rights and Freedoms; copies of the latest interviews with Madam Justice McLachlin; copies of law reviews concerning civil disobedience and public forests; copies of recent relevant judgements. But I will obviously have to defend myself without my papers. Prisoners in these cells are allowed nothing, not even a bra. My bra is taken away along with my shirt. I can only have one item on the upper part of my body, either the shirt or the thin, unlined jacket. I have to make a snap decision. The shirt will look ridiculous without a bra; the jacket will look somewhat better, but it is too low-cut for court without a shirt, especially for a woman my age. I try not to sweat the small stuff when I am in custody, but it seems outrageous that a woman of my age, who is representing herself in court, must appear without a shirt and bra in front of judges, lawyers and hopefully some supporters. I complain. They are used to complaints. They ignore me.

I am given a gown of sorts for the night and I will be allowed a shower in the morning. Dinner is a meat sandwich. I am a vegetarian, I say. Somewhere from the bowels of the unit a tinfoil container of macaroni is unearthed. It is pushed through the opening in the door, not even fully thawed. It's gross. I don't eat it. And neither can I stomach the muffin that comes to me by way of the same slot in the morning. The muffin is 99.9 percent sugar and the coffee might have been hot an hour before it was shoved at me. This is awful. It shouldn't be allowed. Regardless of what people have done, while we are in custody the province has a duty to give us something halfway decent to eat.

The morning shower doesn't materialize, either. They are too short-staffed. Maybe later. So I am brought into court braless, shirt-less, with no make up, hair hastily combed with a communal jail comb. My court papers are held hostage by an officer standing at the end of the prisoner's box, who refuses to give them over to me.

But I am heartened by the familiar faces in the audience. We schmooze each other with smiles and mouthed encouragement. And the judge seems like a decent enough fellow. He asks what I was doing on the capital lawn and I tell him. Okay, he says in effect, but you can't do that; however, I will release you until trial if you sign an order that you won't camp on the legislative lawn. And I say no, sir, I won't do that. Chief Justice McLachlin recently said the law also belongs to the Canadian people and the—

"Yes, well, Mrs. Krawczyk, if you don't agree not to go back and camp then I will have to order that you remain in custody until your trial."

"And we ask for a publication ban on Mrs. Krawczyk," the prose-cutor for the Crown breaks in. This truly alarms me.

"Sir, I want to speak to that—" I begin.

The judge waves me back, as if fearful I will emerge from the risoner's box. He will not give such an order, he assures me.

I decide that this is a good time to talk about the airplane that pris-oners are forced into when we are transported between Victoria and

Vancouver. I am a white-knuckled flyer—in fact, I have a full-blown phobia about flying. I only fly when I must, when a death or severe illness calls me southward, and then I must have a tranquillizer or several stiff drinks. And I'm not a drinker. Drinks don't just make me drunk, they also make me sick. So I try my damnedest to stay off airplanes. And the little transport plane used by the Attorney General for prisoner transfers fills me with terror, as it seems to be stuck together with spit and bandages. It isn't that I'm so afraid of dying; I just don't want to be terrorized in the process.

I tell the judge that the plane used for prisoners is twice as old as I am and so is the pilot. Actually, I don't think the pilot is so old, because while he has white hair, his face is youngish, but I have a point to make here. I do not want to get on that bloody plane. I know it very well from the Clayoquot blockades. A senior sheriff happens to be in the courtroom and the judge says that while he can't give an order, the sheriff has heard my complaint. The judge indicates that I might be allowed to travel to the Burnaby Correctional Centre for Women by ferry. He sets a date for the trial to be held in Victoria, and I am dismissed.

But later, when I am allowed to talk to Bob Moore-Stewart, my legal advisor, we both remember that Mr. Justice Parrett's decision is coming down on September fourteenth and that my lawn-camping charge would be too close to that date, so we need to have it changed. When I am brought back into the courtroom for the date change, I stand before a different judge. This judge just seems to want to make a deal. He tells me I don't have to sign anything; if I will just verbally agree not to camp on the legislative lawn, he will let me go. He says I can picket and leaflet to my heart's desire, I just can't camp. If I will just agree verbally to that ... No, I say, Chief Justice of Canada

Madam Beverley McLachlin just said in a recent interview that the laws of Canada—

But the judge already has the picture. Take her away, he says. Or words to that effect. I get more macaroni for lunch, but at least the promised shower materializes. It has to run for at least five and maybe even ten minutes before it turns hot, but it finally does. Then it shuts off every three seconds or so and I have to press a button to turn it back on. That's to keep people from dying in the shower from one thing or another without staff being alerted, the officer explains to me. Afterward, she brings me a cup of coffee that is actually hot. But the afternoon goes rapidly downhill after that.

It's cold in the cell. I have socks but no shoes. An officer finally brings me a couple of magazines to read; I still don't have my court papers. Most women's magazines fill me with as much horror as the Attorney General's airplane. Women's magazines have become soft porn. Which might be okay if they sailed under that flag, but their pretence of imparting information friendly to women is as absurd as this jail's junk food. What is woman-friendly about emaciated bodies, tortured hair and dress styles, youth the only game in town? Give me a break.

I close the magazine in disgust and do some exercises. Just as the day is thankfully winding down, a man is brought in who will keep me awake most of the night.

Why are the men's cells so close to the women's cells? Men are ten times more belligerent and make ten times the noise. There should be at least ten football fields between the men and the women. And another thing that bugs me about jail is the gender issue. It is considered more normal for men to raise hell than women, so more hell-raising is tolerated from men. A woman raving out of control is considered more unnatural and is punished more severely. I've seen women get pepper-sprayed for a lot less than what this jerk across the way is doing. He's determined that if he can't sleep, then nobody will. Oh, well. I'll just do what Mama always said to do in odious situations: concentrate on the positive. This night, too, will pass, and tomorrow morning I'll be on my way to Burnaby Correctional Centre for Women via a nice ferry ride, out of range of this particular maniac's voice.

Mama and her sayings. How trite they are, how they guide me in spite of my better judgement: Pretty is as pretty does; don't count your chickens; don't cry over spilt milk; a stitch in time; haste makes waste; watch your skirt doesn't ride up; a penny saved; that man can't come to the house unless he talks to your daddy first; don't frown, your face will freeze that way; do you want to turn out like your cousin?; out of the frying pan; look before you leap; he who hesitates is lost; he who fights and runs away lives to fight another day ...

Well, I've certainly lived that last one. I was born with a social conscience all out of proportion to my physical, emotional, financial and intellectual ability to support such a thing. So my life requires a lot of resting in between bouts of activism. I'm unlike my mother, who stayed on a steady, even course of daily goodness and service to others without fits and starts or abrupt beginnings or endings. Mama at least had resisted the impulse to chuck it all and head for the wilderness. Mama, can you hear me? I whisper into the semi-darkness of my cell. Is Barbara with you? And Doris? And Daddy? Do you at last know the final mysteries? Is it what you thought it would be, at least for you? Are you playing a piano duet with your mother the way you thought you would?

In that cold, cramped cell with the tormented male prisoner

yelling down the establishment on the other side of the hall, I suddenly feel my mother's presence and my mind goes back to that summer of two years ago in Mississippi, when Mama was in the intensive
care unit. The cardiologist had come to examine her.

"I'm sorry," he said, taking me aside. "I can't give you much hope.
She's too old for an operation. There's only blood thinners. She may
last the night, she may not."

"What did you tell her?" I asked.

He is tall, older, busy. But not unkind. I can see the sympathy in
his grey eyes. My soul is in the process of becoming temporarily
numbed out. It is an emotional dumbing down; without it even the
strongest of humans would die of grief.

"The truth," he answered. "She took it well. She says she's ready."

"I want to spend the night in her room."

"Certainly. I'll arrange for a recliner."

I thanked him. He left and I peeked back in on Mama. She was
asleep again. I decided to do three things while she was asleep: eat,
make phone calls and see Aunt Gladys. I would see Aunt Gladys first.
I had to think of some way to tell her about Mama. But when I got to
Aunt Gladys' room it become apparent almost immediately that she
had lost her mind.

But she did recognize me.

"Betty, I'm so glad you're here. Ain't those your little tap dancing
shoes underneath that chest of drawers there?"

I look. There is nothing under the small white metal chest.

"I don't think so, Aunt Gladys ..."

"They are so. I can see them from here. Where's Bug?"

"Uh, she's resting ..."

"Well, she better get here. Doris' boys are coming to play music.

Doris is going to sing. And we can dance. Do you know where my tap shoes are? Maybe Bug forgot to bring them."

She pushed the meal tray back and tried to get out of bed. I rushed to her side and pressed the nurse's buzzer.

"Aunt Gladys, don't get up yet," I said firmly. "You haven't finished your lunch. Look, you've left your potato and most of your chicken."

"I wouldn't put that chicken in hog slop. The potato, either. These cooks here are a disgrace to Louisiana."

"You're in Mississippi, Aunt Gladys."

"Am I? What am I doing in Mississippi? Never mind, I want my tap shoes."

Just then the nurse answered my summons.

"Miss Gladys, you can't go anywhere right now," the nurse said as she pulled the lunch tray back into position, which hemmed Aunt Gladys in.

"Yes, I can, can't I, darling?" Aunt Gladys asked, appealing to me. "Tell the nurse I have to find my tap shoes. Those are yours, under that cabinet. Doris is coming, too. She'll sing and we'll dance, won't we darling?"

Darling. The little endearment that Aunt Gladys had used so casually in her life to both men and women was scary when applied to me. That more than anything else, more even than reference to my long-dead sister and her tap shoes (which had been retired for at least forty years), let me know that Aunt Gladys had finally burst through to another zone altogether. A very scary one. The nurse came to the rescue. "Miss Gladys, your doctor is on her way to see you. She's going to be mightily displeased when she see you've hardly touched your lunch. You can tell her about the tap shoes. I'll help you with your lunch, but I'm going to have to ask your niece to leave."

The nurse turned to me with a bright, professional smile. "Would you mind stopping by the nurses' station? The head nurse wants to talk to you."

And I wanted to talk to her. "Is Aunt Gladys' confusion perma-nent?" I asked the head nurse at the desk. She was a big black woman who carried herself with dignity.

"We don't know," she answered. "Can you tell us when her con-fusion started?"

"Just since her fall. There was a gradual decline in her memory be-fore, but nothing like this. She's lost touch with reality."

"Yes. Her doctor will be examining her thoroughly, of course. I just wondered where you were with it, if there was anything you might add when Dr. Hartrix comes."

"Just that there seems to have been a sudden, quantum leap in her loss of memory. Do you think it might just be temporary?"

"I don't know. But I'll report your observations to the doctor. She might want to talk to you herself."

Visiting with Aunt Gladys being out of the question, I decided to call Ray Allen and Carol. Ray Allen picked up the phone.

"Do you think we should head back to Phoenix tonight?" he asked.

"Maybe. If you have to go there before you come here."

"Yes. We need to bank and get different clothes."

"Then head back," I said. "The doctor doesn't give Mama long."

"Okay. Are you all right?"

"I'll manage. Did I mention that Aunt Gladys has lost her mind entirely?"

"No," he answered. There was a little silence. I knew he was thinking the same thing I was but he was the one who said it. "How can you tell?"

Typical Shiver comment. When one is faced with disaster, a moral choice usually presents itself: One can curse God and die, or take a leap into the spiritual cosmos. The Shivers short-circuit both options and try to joke their way into survival—often in the most macabre manner possible.

"Well, we could give her a regular pair of dice," I offered, "and see how long it takes her to swap them for a loaded pair."

"Or we could introduce her to the meanest, most crooked, penniless old white man in Mississippi and see how long it takes her to marry him," Ray Allen countered.

"The doctor has already suggested a nursing home," I said.

"We'll drive back to Phoenix tonight and try to get a plane out tomorrow night. We'll see you soon."

So far, so good. Down to the cafeteria. Too late. It was closed. I made do with wrapped sandwiches and pop and potato chips from a vending machine. When I got back to Mama's room, she was awake and wearing her glasses.

"Betty, don't look so scared," she said when I took my seat beside her. "I'm ninety-five years old. You know I have to die sometime."

"Just not right now," I answered.

"Oh, pooh. You just don't want to be the matriarch."

"That's right, Mama. I don't have the calling. Besides, I'm not even a Southerner anymore."

"Yes, you are. Don't you pay any attention to Gladys about that."

"I was born in Mississippi," she added after a moment. Her voice was softer and lower than usual, but firm enough. Her voice had always sounded young; over the phone she could still sound like a young girl. I pressed her hand to my cheek. "And I'm going to die in Mississippi," she went on. "And I'll be buried in Louisiana beside my husband and my daughter, and you just remember that all your folks are Southerners and it don't matter how long you live up there with all those Canadians, you're still a Southerner. And don't be afraid of death. It comes to us all."

"I know, Mama."

"And I'll see my daughter and your daughter. So stop worrying."

"I'm not worrying, Mama. It's just that nobody will ever love me the way you do," I whispered against the wonderful, work-worn hand that lay so unnaturally still against my cheek. "You always loved me no matter what. Even when I did the craziest things. Who is going to love me like that now? Nobody, that's who."

"You have your kids. They love you."

"But they only see me one way, as mother …"

"And what do you know of me except as mother?"

"Oh, I don't know …" I broke off, sobbing into her hand.

"Betty, remember where I put the key for the box."

"I remember. I'll do everything like you said. The insurance papers and all."

"And the blue dress. For my funeral. And don't forget the white lace top."

"I won't forget. I promise."

"Betty, I'm tired now. I'm going back to sleep."

"All right, Mama."

I sat there, trying not to impose my grief on her in her last hours, until she drifted off. She seemed to be breathing strongly and her colour wasn't all that bad. When the male nurse came in, I told him I'd be right outside making phone calls.

"Your mother is a very funny lady," he said as I was leaving. "She asked me what people ate where I came from and I told her lots of rice and fish and chicken and hot peppers, and she said the Philippines must be full of Cajuns."

"And are they?" I asked.

He laughed quietly, so as not to waken Mama. The man had a happy heart.

Just outside the unit I was relieved to find the phone booth empty. First I called Geraldine to please go check on Sweetie. Then I left messages for all of the kids and stopped to pick up another coffee from the vending machine on my way back to the unit. I sipped the coffee by Mama's bedside, watching her sleep. She looked peaceful enough, except that once again she was sleeping with her glasses on. She never did that, so I reached over and removed the glasses. She didn't stir. When I placed the glasses on the bedside table, I noticed a spider.

He was only a very tiny spider, but what was he doing in here, I wondered. This unit had been scrubbed within an inch of its life. Probably the spider had been brought in on someone's clothes. Maybe I had brought it in myself. I no longer killed spiders or allowed anyone around me to kill them. Not since the dream I had about spiders shortly after Barbara died.

I dreamed I was in the crawl space underneath an old house and it was slimy and dark and evil-smelling. I wanted out. And daylight was shining through a round opening at one end of the crawl space. Ah, escape! I crawled toward the light on my hands and knees. The sunshine looked so wonderful and I was so happy that I'd soon be out of this awful place but when I got right up to the escape hatch I saw all the spiders. There were dozens of them gathered right around the opening in the wall. Every time I inched forward they would activate and jump about in a very threatening manner. When I pulled back, their activity would subside. And then I saw the mother of them all—a huge black spider with a body as big as my fist, hanging right over the opening. There was no way to get out. I was being held prisoner by spiders. I sank back into the crawl space, utterly defeated.

I woke up crying after that dream. Later in the morning I idly opened one of Barbara's books on mythology. It wasn't a subject that usually interested me a great deal so I just flipped through, reading randomly. A chapter on spider myths caught my eye. In some African myths Grandmother Spider brings wisdom. She goes around the world appearing to humans in different circumstances, accompanied by her grandsons, teaching humans how to be human. I figured the dream had been a visitation from Grandmother Spider and her grandsons, and thereafter I looked upon spiders differently.

I decided to capture this little fellow and take him outside. There was a glass by the sink and I pulled a stiff piece of notepaper from my purse. Holding the two objects, I hovered and waited to strike. But the spider seemed to divine my intent to capture it because he executed a couple of lightning-quick darts from side to side and then disappeared underneath the tabletop.

Temporarily defeated, I returned to my chair and coffee. The trouble with spiders, I was thinking, was that they have such terrible body language. In fact, their body language is so repulsive to humans that even the most harmless of the species give people the willies. But Mama wasn't afraid of spiders or bats or even snakes. No creepy-crawly thing stood a chance around our house. She just didn't tolerate them. She especially hated chicken hawks, though. There were lots of chicken hawks in Louisiana, and they all seemed to know when Mama's hens were coming out into the yard with their newest broods. When a hawk would swoop down and seize a baby chick in its talons, Mama would scream and throw rocks and even cuss. Well, for her it was cussing. She would damn the hawk's soul to hell and back. And then she would try to explain to any of us kids in the vicinity that she didn't really mean it.

"Chicken hawks are God's creatures, too," she explained to me one afternoon after a hawk had swooped down and captured a fuzzy little chick that had been innocently scratching around with its siblings while its mother chased a grasshopper. "They have to take food home to their chicks, too."

"But it seems so cruel, Mama," I remember saying. I was about eight or nine and just coming to realize that we, ourselves, ate of the flesh at our little farm.

"I know, Sugar Baby. But it's nature's way."

"But why, Mama? Why couldn't everybody just eat grass and then nobody's kids would have to be eaten by anything else? Why couldn't it be arranged like that?"

"You'll have to ask God."

"I can't ask God. I don't know where he is."

"He's in you."

"No, He's not either. I don't want Him in me."

Mama laughed and sat down on the back step. Her thick, wavy dark hair had escaped from the bun on the top of her head and was tumbling down her back. I sat down beside her.

The mother hen was still nervous, casting anxious glances to the sky with one side of her head this way and that, but she resumed nervously pecking on the ground with her remaining chicks around her.

"God's in everything," Mama said. "He's in you and me and the chickens and the chicken hawks and the corn and turnip greens and okra and the pigs—"

"Pigs? God's in the pork chops?"

"Yes."

"And the watermelons?"

"Yes."

"Well … what about bad people?"

"God's in them, too."

"Then why are they bad?"

"They haven't learned any better yet."

"Then how come the preacher says some people are going to hellfire?"

"Because the preacher hasn't learned any better yet."

"Really?"

"Really."

"What about Daddy? He says he believes in hellfire."

"Well, your daddy can believe whatever he wants and I'll believe what I want. And you can believe what you want. I believe that God is good. A God that's good wouldn't make a hellfire to put people in, now would He?"

"No," I answered, leaning against her. We were both barefoot but Mama's print housedress was starched and ironed. Her body was warm but the dress material felt cool against my skin. A few tendrils of hair around her face made Shirley Temple curls and I stuck my finger in one of them. My own hair was straight and I was fascinated with my mother's curly hair. The late summer sun was waning and the air was beginning to cool. Butterflies were making their last forays into the wild roses straggling along the fence, and the faint breeze was sweet with a hint of rain. A deep happiness filled my being. The world was good. There was no hellfire and even the chicken hawks had God in them.

At the moment, though, I was being confronted by the tiny spider on Mama's bedside table in the intensive care unit. He peeked out from the underside of the little table, hung there for a moment and then, deciding it must be safe enough, crawled over the edge until he was right side up. Then he paused. He wasn't rushing to explore the new terrain. Was he simply assessing the situation or did he have to wait a bit until his eyes and senses adjusted from the upside down position? But my attention was diverted from the spider by a sound from Mama.

I turned my head to see her sitting straight up in bed. "Mama? What's the matter?" I asked, instantly alarmed at her appearance. Her face was flushed and when her eyes met mine there was no recognition. Before I could stop her she began tearing the IV needles out of her hand and arm.

I jumped to my feet. "Mama, stop it!" I cried. "What are you doing?"

"Get this mess out of here!" she demanded, flinging the tapes and bandages onto the bed. Her hand was bleeding and her eyes were red and sunken into her skull. There was no recognition in them. "Get this mess out!" she yelled right into my face.

I ran to the door. "Nurse!" I screamed at the top of my voice. "Nurse!" One good thing about having a hog-calling voice like mine is that it isn't easy to ignore. In fact, it was much better than a buzzer. The nurse came running. She was an older white woman from the bayous.

"Oh, Miz Shiver, we can't have this," she said firmly as she grasped one of the needles in Mama's hand and pulled it the rest of the way out.

"I don't want this mess," Mama insisted, looking wildly around the room. I went to her but her gaze slid past me, fixed on the nurse. "Did you stir the beans?" she demanded.

"I'm going to do that right away," the nurse said, cleaning needle and bandage debris from the bed and disposing of it all in the waste-basket.

"Yes, you better tend to it. You let them beans burn last time. Poppa was mad. And did anybody milk the cow?"

"Yes, ma'am. That cow's done been milked."

"Good," Mama said, leaning back a little in the bed. "I want some clabber. I'm going to make some clabber biscuits. Nothing's better than clabber biscuits. That's what Poppa says."

"Ain't it the truth? You lie back down, Miz Shiver, and rest. I'll call you when the clabber's ready."

"Mind you do now."

"Yes, ma'am."

Satisfied, Mama closed her glazed eyes and sank back into the hospital pillows. This wasn't good. This was definitely not good. Poppa? That's what Mama called her father. And she was thinking the nurse was the hired help. And she couldn't place me at all.

"I'll call her doctor," the nurse whispered on her way out with the wastebasket. "And I'll be right back."

Is this the way you're going? I asked silently of the old woman on the bed. Feverish, out of it, no longer even recognizing me, your only daughter left on this earth?

◆

The city jail cells in Victoria have suddenly fallen silent. I open my eyes. Has the deranged man who has been yelling all night finally given out? I believe he has. There are only the little scuffling noises of people moving around down the hall, the faint sound of a covered cough. I have no idea what time it is. They have taken my watch, and my cell door is, of course, locked. Perhaps I can sleep, whatever the time. No sooner have I entertained the thought than someone is at my door with lukewarm coffee and a sugar muffin. What a dreadful place this is! Perhaps I can catch a few winks going over on the ferry. I am dressed and ready when the sheriffs come to transport me back to Vancouver.

"You'll be flying," the sheriff's deputy says.

"No, I won't," I say firmly. "I'm to go over on the ferry. I don't fly."

"It says here you're flying with the others. Your name's on the list."

"Then it's a mistake. I don't fly. Check with your superior."

The sheriff's deputy goes away. She returns after a moment. She has a message from the sheriff. "Sheriff says if you don't want to fly then you can sign the undertaking and you'll be released."

I am stunned. This is blackmail. I have to perjure myself in order to get out of flying in that damn plane. It must be against the law for the sheriff or the Attorney General or anyone in charge of prisoners to make a non flyer fly or else perjure herself. I can't believe it. But I will not give in to this. I am flying under the greatest of protest, I say. And I wonder if I can sue. Oh, I would love to sue the sheriff's office and the Attorney General's office for forcing me to do this!

We prisoners are not only leg-shacked and handcuffed for the flight, but also waist-shackled. A steel chain is put around each person's waist and hooked onto the plane seat. If the plane went down we would have absolutely no chance of escaping burning wreckage or a watery grave. How can a civilized country transport prisoners in this fashion? I try to centre myself during the flight, to go deep inside myself, to block out all external sensation. My concentration is broken by my awareness of two Native high school girls from Ucluelet. They are also shackled and chained. They know my daughter Rose Mary, who teaches in Ucluelet, and my son-in-law Jim is one girl's attorney. The novelty of the coincidence helps to keep me occupied. I lecture them and admonish them to be good when they get back home and they promise they will be.

The flight over, I am processed back into Burnaby Correctional Centre for Women. At least my feet are on the ground. And my legal papers are finally returned to me. But my address to the court on sentencing has disappeared, lost in the shuffle. I'll have to write a new one. I'm in a different unit this time and so far there is no double-bunking, but I have learned to take nothing for granted in this place. I get busy with the writing. There is less than a week until Mr. Justice Parrett returns to pronounce judgement and to sentence us.

I do unit maintenance in the mornings. That is, I help scrub down the joint. After lunch we are locked down for half an hour and I don't have a regular job description for the afternoon yet. So I am free, relatively speaking. I read, write, try to think. None of it is easy in the midst of ruined and broken lives. Surrounded by guards, some of whom are decent in their attitudes toward prisoners, a few who are not, and inmates making mostly futile attempts to reclaim lost children, lost relationships, even lost pets, thinking is difficult. The dichotomy between prison as oppressive punishment and prison as refuge is constantly open for examination. At least the women are physically safe— safe from the violence of the streets, from the violence of their boyfriends and pimps, from the violence of the arresting police, from the violence of addictions.

For the ones who are in for long-term incarceration, I would ask, What's the point? Most of the murderers here killed in passion or after prolonged abuse. Incarceration as we know it is, in my opinion, a crime against nature and the human spirit. The addicts belong in extended health care facilities with proper diet and exercise and hope for the future; the murderers belong in positions in the community where they can exercise the soul-cleansing practice of restitution. In spite of the fact that I witness little daily acts of care and compassion among the inmates and staff, incarceration brings out the worst in everybody. To guard another human being in order to see that her freedom is curtailed is a disgraceful thing. It is akin to slavery. It elevates one over the other in obscene ways that degrade the mental and spiritual condition of both, and it should not be practised except in the most extreme circumstances, such as with serial murderers. Even then the consciousness of the guards should be monitored at all times so that they remain acutely aware that while their job is necessary and honourable, it is also extremely desensitizing. In fact, perhaps there should be strict limits placed on how long anyone can serve in the capacity of guarding another human being.

◆

At last the date I have been waiting for, September 14, 2000, arrives. Today Mr. Justice Parrett will give his judgement on the first Elaho

trial. When I am escorted out of the cells in the Supreme Court building and walk into the courtroom itself I am heartened to see it's full of
supporters and newspeople. As I walk toward the prisoner's box I
pick out my daughter Marian in the crowd, sitting with a few close
friends. Barbara Ellen explained to me once the secret of how not to
get dizzy in ballet while whirling around on point. The trick is to spot
something in the immediate vicinity and concentrate on that one
thing. I have spotted Marian and my friends. Even when I must turn
my head to face the judge from the prisoner's box, I will see my
daughter and friends in my mind's eye if my head starts whirling with
emotion.

The court convenes. The judge speaks. And speaks and speaks. I
don't agree with much of anything he is saying. The core of his rea-
soning is that we broke a court order in the Elaho and that is truly all
that matters. After denying Robbie's and my submissions for a stay of
proceedings, he begins the actual sentencing. He starts with Barney,
listing his sins in detail. We all know Mr. Justice Parrett finds Barney
reprehensible. It's somewhat odd, really. Barney is not the master
brain dictator of evil in the woods the judge thinks he is. Can the
judge only define us in terms of military hierarchy? Of course he finds
Barney guilty of criminal contempt of court. Then Mr. Justice Parrett
moves on to Christopher Keats. Keats is also found guilty of criminal
contempt. Chris Nolan is next. Criminal contempt. Guilty. At this
point Christopher Keats disrupts the proceedings and is removed
from the court. Dennis Porter is next. He's not so easy for the judge
to pin down, as he went out to the Elaho as a reporter. However, he is
still found guilty of civil contempt of court. Rick McCallion is also
found guilty of the lesser charge of civil contempt. Justin Paine is
found guilty of criminal contempt, as is Reasha Wolfe. Mr. Justice

Parrett doesn't pronounce Camille Willicome guilty of anything. He says: "In the end, I am left, however, with a reasonable doubt as to her knowledge of the order and its terms in light of the whole of the evidence." Good. Camille was only in the Elaho accidentally. I'm next. And last.

"What can I say about Betty Krawczyk?" Mr. Justice Parrett asks. "She at least has the courage of her convictions. She has never wavered from her open intention to force on others the task of arresting her and putting her in jail. Her goal in ensuring this end is to use her appearance, her age and her willingness to speak out as a vehicle to obtain media and public expression. She openly advocates public defiance of the law and the orders, and asserts the goals in which she believes. I have no doubt of her sincerity in those beliefs, as I have no doubt as to the result I am forced to impose. The evidence against Betty Krawczyk is overwhelming. One could quite literally look at virtually any segment of the evidence involving her and find proof of the four constituent elements of criminal contempt. She is a person who at no time sought to conceal her actions, the reasons for them or the impact of them. The result of those actions gives me no pleasure, for Ms. Krawczyk is both personable and likable, but over the many days we have been together in this courtroom and my perhaps feeble attempts to explain the process to her, I see no likelihood that she will swerve from the course she has chartered [sic] for herself. I find Betty Krawczyk guilty of criminal contempt of court."

Well, there you go. Mr. Justice Parrett will reserve the actual sentencing for tomorrow. So I have all evening and all night to stew about it. One thing about already being in jail is that the shock of coming into the institution is over. I'm already here. What can Mr. Justice Parrett do to me? More of the same, that's all, and I've tested the waters, I'm stronger than the system. Might I have some sort of built-in talent for jail that it holds no particular terrors for me? I doubt it. I'd say the explanation is much more ominous.

Any woman living in a male-dominated culture like ours is already in jail. Her life-giving functions are devalued; her children can be thrown to the winds; she and her children must be always on the alert from physical attacks from men; a woman's very sex is subjected to contempt; her superior skills of cooperation and mediation are treated with scorn; and the more work she performs to keep the society glued together, the more unselfishly she gives, the more basely she is treated.

Ours is still a Madonna/whore society, and neither is respected. The whore, if she can stay unaddicted, might come out with a little more money, but her self-esteem is lower than the average Madonna's pocketbook. If the Madonna is on her own with children, she ceases to be a Madonna and becomes a drain on the public purse. At which point she may consider whoring to be spared the humiliation of begging a grudging society for sustenance. In prison the veneer of society is stripped away and one can truly see, starkly revealed, the thinly concealed contempt for women this society holds.

But while this pervasive contempt may keep women down, it is a double-edged sword. Men as a group can't hold the attitudes they do toward women without deliberately denying fundamental truths about the universe. And no race or species will survive long in historical terms without a reasonably accurate assessment of objective truths. So I am at home in prison because I have been in prison all of my life; jail is only another expression of that. However, deep inside myself I am free. I am free because my thoughts, my allegiances, my loves are my own, so I am not afraid of physical confinement. Somehow I would like to convey this to the judge before being sentenced in the morning. It will not make any difference to him—I know that. But it will make a difference to me if I can manage to express myself credibly. And there is something about Mr. Justice Parrett that is all of a piece. He has a certain integrity, in the sense that he has consistency of thought and action. His remarks and judgements might as well come from the mouth of the Pope: This you may do, this you may not do; there are no mitigating circumstances. We white men have spoken; go eat dirt, if you have to, but obey. Well, maybe that's a little harsh.

After lockdown for the night, I sit at my cell desk. And my thoughts turn once again to that last summer with my mother when she was in intensive care, supposedly breathing her last ...

◆

"Is your mother still sleeping?" the Philippine nurse asked softly from behind my chair.

"Yes," I answered, and quickly moved around so he could get to Mama's side. He did a brief check of her vital functions.

"The doctor ordered that the medications be discontinued until she arrives. She thinks your mother might be having a reaction to the medications, or ..."

I nodded. I knew very well what the "or" meant.

Discontinuing the medications didn't seem to bother Mama. She slept on. Dr. Hartrix arrived fifteen minutes later. She examined Mama and then motioned me outside the room.

"We can put the IVs back in or leave them out," she said coldly. "It's up to you."

I felt a surge of revulsion for this woman.

"Leave them out," I conceded. "My mother doesn't want them."

"I think that's best," the doctor answered. Her expression softened and she gave a smug little smile. Why not? Her superior doctor's judgement had been confirmed. "I'll be here for a couple of hours and I'll look in again before I leave."

I went back to Mama's bedside. While I was out somebody had replaced the straight-backed chair with a recliner. Mama was snoring ever so softly. I got as comfortable as I could, and dropped right into a deep sleep. I woke up once and leaned over Mama. She was still breathing regularly. And then I popped right off again. This time when I woke, it was with Mama's voice ringing in my ears.

"Betty! Betty! Wake up, it's daylight."

I fairly jerked awake, instantly ready for disaster. But no. For a change, it was something good. Mama had come back to her senses.

"Okay, Mama," I said quickly, getting up and taking her hand. "Mama, do you know where you are?"

She peered up at me in the semi-darkness of the room. "What's wrong with you, girl? Of course I know where I am. I'm in the hospital, boob. That doctor said I was going to die, but I didn't, did I? At least not yet. Do you know where that crazy nurse put my glasses?"

"Yes, Mama," I said happily, opening the bedside drawer. "They're right here. They're just right here, waiting for you."

Happy, happy, happy. Mama was going to make the hundred mark after all.

Three weeks later we were well into moving her and her most precious possessions back to Louisiana. Mama had agreed to move back into her apartment in Baton Rouge with the grandkids, and Aunt

Gladys was going into a nursing home nearby. I was packing up the last two cardboard boxes when Mama asked about my son Mike.

"Oh, he's out in the northern Manitoba bush somewhere."

"How come he left the cabin in the Clayoquot? Didn't he like it?"

"Mike always finds a good reason for leaving a place. He's very restless. Always has been. Let's see ... this time I think he mentioned it was because the women on the island were all either virgins, veterinarians or vegetarians, and some were all three. He's pretty sexist, you know."

"He's a good boy," Mama said firmly.

Boy? Mike was pushing fifty.

"He's mellowing," I said. Mike was hardly a boy, but he would still start any project armed with next to nothing but enthusiasm, which caused him to attempt the most outlandish things. He couldn't read a note of music but he wrote an entire opera; he refused to fly if he could help it but was well into building an airplane before he conceded that there might be a little more to the project than a set of plans. He looked always with the eyes of a child: The world was ever new, possibilities were ever endless, he trod over the earth's crust painting and sculpting as he went, and when he got to the sea he took to the boats ...

"And he's not a drunkard," Mama went on. "I guess that's all an old woman can really wish for is that her grandchildren stay sober and out of jail."

She paused, laughing at me. "Of course, I have a daughter who's a jailbird."

Actually Mama supported my Clayoquot protest. It was the first one I'd been involved in that she supported unequivocally. She believed whatever men in power said about most matters and when she didn't, she forgave them for being stupid, but clearcutting old-growth forests was about as crazy to her as it was to me.

When I left her two weeks later, Mama was firmly installed back in her old apartment, in her old stomping grounds. She looked well and seemed satisfied with the arrangement, and she went to visit Aunt Gladys almost every day. But perhaps the move was too much. I had barely been home three weeks when my nephew called with the message that Mama had collapsed and died on the way to the hospital.

I caught the first plane out to Baton Rouge. Two of my nephews and their wives met me at the airport. It was around eight o'clock in the evening when we arrived at the old house. The kitchen was full of women. Relatives, friends, food. A frenzied involvement with food was going on: scraping, dicing, paring, mixing, stirring. The Cajun contingent of the family was obviously in charge of the food preparation. I was offered nourishment, but declined. It was all too much. I was dazed. There were more relatives in and out of the living room, the den, people I hadn't seen in years. The funeral would be at two in the afternoon. Afterwards all the kin would come back to the house for dinner. Ray Allen and Carol would arrive early in the morning. The two other grandsons and their wives would arrive around midnight. I couldn't stay up that long. I was exhausted. I retired at ten and slept in Mama's bed.

Aunt Gladys woke me up the morning of Mama's funeral. When I opened my eyes, she was peering anxiously down into my face.

"Betty, wake up! I'm going back to Canada with you!"

Chapter Thirteen

Going back to Canada with me? With me? Aunt Gladys? The very notion of such a thing revved up my fight-or-flight responses and I fairly hopped out of bed.

"Aunt Gladys, you can't do that," I said, taking her arm gently but firmly. "Why, the people at the Manor would be right put out if you left now."

"Naw, they wouldn't. They don't give a shit. Bug wants me to go back to Canada with you."

I searched her eyes, trying to gauge if she was really that confused at the moment or if she was trying to trick me. Her eyes held mine in a glistening, unblinking gaze. But however spaced out she might be, I couldn't let her entertain the notion, even for a moment, that she had the option of going home with me.

"Aunt Gladys, Mama is dead," I said patiently. "Anyway, you never agreed with half of what Mama said when she was alive. Remember how you two used to squabble over your father? Mama said your Poppa was a mean ole man."

Aunt Gladys immediately swelled up like a happy toad.

"Bug didn't have no right to say that! Poppa was a good man. He favoured me, that's all. That's why Bug says mean things about him. Because Poppa favoured me."

"Well, there you are," I said conversationally. "Have you had breakfast yet?"

She blinked at me. "Breakfast? Oh hell, I don't know. Have I?"

"We'll ask somebody in the kitchen," I said, slipping on Mama's flowery housecoat, which was still lying across the foot of the bed. "I smell coffee."

The contingent in the kitchen was still going strong, only the players had changed. Jean's wife, the lady of the house, had gone to bed at four in the morning. A different battalion of nieces, cousins, grand-nieces, neighbours and friends of friends wandered in and out, bringing more food, more drinks, more flowers …

I was told Aunt Gladys had eaten breakfast already, but I grabbed a couple of rolls just out of the oven to be on the safe side. I juggled the plate of rolls, two glasses of iced tea and one cup of the impossibly strong, black, bitter, thick goo that still held the Confederate flag high in the face of the more reasonable coffees of the world. Aunt Gladys followed me out to what used to be the back porch. The coffee was for her. I settled for the iced tea. My blood wasn't the only thing that had thinned from my extended stay in more northern climes. My stomach lining had thinned, too, so I willingly relinquished the coffee.

Ah, the changes that time hath wrought, I thought as I surveyed the damage done to the erstwhile screened porch by artificial light. Why, I could remember when this space was truly just a screened porch. It had offered shade, comfortable chairs and a big fan. There had been a weeping willow on the other side of the walkway. The tree had indeed been remarkable, as all weeping willows are. The slightest breeze would send its tendrils swaying into a rippling, mesmerizing dance.

The willow had disappeared to make room for the expanded porch and the huge ceramic pots sitting on concrete pillars. The ratty, old-fashioned wicker chairs had been replaced by colourful hardened Jell-O moulded into the shape of chairs. They were chair impostors; I didn't like them. And the wall that had separated the porch from the rest of the house was now a continuous sheet of glass, broken only by sliding glass doors. And the plain wooden floors had been covered over with big squares of glossy black and white tiles that extended inside to a spacious all-purpose room that could house a small convention. Which it will do this afternoon after Mama's funeral.

I was not looking forward to the funeral. And I would never come back to this city, or to Louisiana or Mississippi, for that matter. I was married twice in this city, five of my children were born here, but I was sure I would never come here again. Other than the joy-filled memories of my children as youngsters, there was too much pain here. The pain of race. The pain of religion. The pain of man on woman. The pain of poverty. The pain of rebellion. Personal pain from personal struggles.

"Betty, where's Rex?" Aunt Gladys asked suddenly, peering around the edge of the porch.

Rex who? What was she talking about? And then I remembered: her dog. He'd been dead almost twenty years.

"Rex died, Aunt Gladys," I answered. "You had him put down, remember?"

"Did I do that? Why, I don't remember. What was wrong with him?" Her eyes searched my face, puzzled.

"He was old and sick. He couldn't walk anymore. Rex was very sick. You did the right thing, Aunt Gladys."

Aunt Gladys nodded, but she still didn't seem satisfied. She refused one of the buns, her stomach evidently aware it had had food, even if her mind couldn't recall. She just sipped the black coffee.

"Maybe I should have called in the voodoo woman for Rex," she said after a moment. I opened one of the buns. The top was browned and crusty and brushed with butter. Parker House rolls. Mama used to make them on special occasions.

"Why?" I asked. "The voodoo woman didn't do you any good with Leno."

"With who?"

"With Leno. Your fifth husband."

"My fifth husband wasn't Leno."

"Then who was?" I asked, and bit into the bun. Delicious. Almost as good as Mama's.

"I didn't have any fifth husband. I don't know anybody named Leno."

"Good," I said. He wasn't worth remembering, I thought, not the way he treated you. Leno had been younger than Aunt Gladys, with eyes as big and brown as hers, white teeth, and a strong, stocky, muscular body. No money, of course. But he did work in Aunt Gladys' business. He did do that. And he also, after a few years, got involved with Daisy, Aunt Gladys' best friend.

Aunt Gladys had about as much luck with girlfriends as she did with husbands. This girlfriend was a zinger. Plump, pretty, fast-talking, she just waltzed Leno right out from under Aunt Gladys' nose. But it wasn't easy. It took Daisy a solid year and a half to accomplish her mission. During this time Leno was dividing his time between Daisy and Aunt Gladys. Or trying to. Aunt Gladys suffered. She became gaunt and irritable. In desperation, she went to back of town, as the black ghetto was called then, and sought out the services of the voodoo woman.

Lots of white people did this when they needed a little stronger medicine than the white Christian God seemed willing to deliver. And at least Aunt Gladys' visits to the voodoo woman seemed to cheer her.

Mama's reaction to all this was swift. "My God, Gladys, you aren't trying to kill Daisy, are you?" she asked, horrified.

"Of course not," Aunt Gladys replied. "I just want to make Leno stop wanting Daisy. These charms are just to close up her snapping pussy—"

"Don't talk to me like that," Mama admonished sternly, but Aunt Gladys wasn't up for sisterly criticism in the humiliating situation she found herself in. She fancied everybody was talking about her and her triangle and feeling sorry for her, but it would have surprised me if anyone felt much pity for her since she had taken Leno away from his first wife and bragged about it. Now she remembered this and didn't want to, so she took it out on Mama.

"Gladys, be reasonable," Mama said. "Why do you even want a man who wants another woman, who is living with another woman half the time?"

Aunt Gladys answered, "Shut up, Bug, you don't know anything about this, all you have known is one man in your entire life. Leave me alone." Then Aunt Gladys went on, humming happily as she collected the little things the voodoo woman said she needed to put a hex on Leno's desire for Daisy's pussy: a few strands of Daisy's hair, a button, a scarf.

But the voodoo didn't work. The snapping pussy kept snapping and it snapped Leno away from Aunt Gladys forever. Aunt Gladys was devastated at the time, and now she can't even remember the man's name. But she can remember the name of the dog she had twenty years before. Well, the dog probably gave her a lot more happiness, I thought to myself as I started on another Parker House roll. The rolls would hold me until after the funeral. I didn't want to eat again before the service because I had almost fainted at my sister's funeral.

Southern funerals: emotions raw, whipped even rawer by Southern preachers. What better time, they figure, to suck in new converts and rededications. Quickly, while the mourners are stunned by the fact of death and fearful of their own. Now's the time to preach the gospel. And to bolster the message, there was all the glory-going-to-heaven hallelujah music. At Doris' funeral the preacher got totally wound up. We should all be dancing with joy, he hollered, our sister is meeting her saviour face to face. While we, the living, are left here on earth to cry, cry, cry, heaven is jumping up and down with happy surprise to welcome our sister. Then this theme burst forth from the hallelujah band on stage, complete with horns and guitars and keyboard and drums—oh yes, the drums, the drummer was fairly possessed with the Holy Spirit.

And then Doris' oldest son Eddie, who was a petroleum engineer but also a lay preacher in a fundamentalist church, got up with his sweet wife and talked about his mother and how many people she had helped in her job as a nurse. It was all true; all one had to do was look around the overflowing church to know she was loved and appreciated. Then the preacher went on to talk about how Doris trusted in the power of the Lord ... which may have been true, but she also trusted mightily in vodka and pills. But in that moment of time with Doris' son and his wife testifying with tears rolling down their cheeks, I was mesmerized. And then, when the preacher took the pulpit again and assured me personally that I would see my sister again in heaven if I would only accept the Lord Jesus Christ as my saviour, why, I was plumb tempted ...

If that was all it took to see Doris again, to look into her beautiful eyes, the large, slightly slanted blue-green eyes I had envied so, eyes that were replicated in my daughter Margaret's heart-shaped face so that I could never look at her without seeing my sister as a young girl, oh, yes, accepting the notion of Jesus Christ seemed a small thing, a very small thing, oh, if only I could think it true. But I couldn't.

As hard as I tried, as hard even as I wished I could, because it would solve a lot of problems for me ... I couldn't. Christianity is a world view that tells you why you are here (you are here to serve the Lord) and what your duties are (your duties are to obey His dictates), and if you cann't do this, and you strike out on your own, so to speak, you are going to have a much harder row to hoe. But even knowing all this full well, and even with all the music and the singing and crying and the joyful hugging and patting and urging and pleading, "Come home, sister, give your heart to the Lord, come in and join the magic circle" ... I couldn't.

Feeling faint from all the emotion, I got up and went outside for some fresh air. And I almost stumbled over my brother, who was seeking the same. Years later on one of my trips down South, Mama and I were discussing funerals and I told her I wanted to be cremated. She wanted to know why and I said all the usual stuff about being returned more directly to the earth, it was cleaner, cheaper, less fuss. And I mentioned how distressing Doris' funeral had been for me. And tomorrow will be more of the same, I was thinking now on the porch of Doris' house. An evangelistic preacher with all the attending horrors. The rolls and iced tea would keep me from fainting.

"I hate that preacher," I said out loud.

"What?"

"The preacher. The one who preached Doris' funeral. I guess he's going to preach Mama's funeral, too."

"Bug ain't having no preacher," Aunt Gladys said.

I laughed. Her response just sounded funny. But my laughing riled Aunt Gladys up.

"Why you laughing like a fool? Bug ain't having no preacher. She told me. She said it was a present to you. She wrote it down. The boys have the paper."

"What?" I asked, looking at my poor addled aunt.

But just then Ray Allen and Carol arrived and came to the porch looking for us. The day's schedule swallowed us up. People had to be picked up from airports and bus stations, phones rang incessantly, car pools were arranged, we were dressed and somehow I arrived at the funeral home at the appointed time with the others. At least the service was to be in the funeral home chapel. That in itself would force some restraint on the preacher's evangelism.

I stood at the chapel door in a daze, with Ray Allen and Carol and Aunt Gladys receiving condolences from friends and relatives as they entered. Someone had found a wheelchair for Aunt Gladys. When the crowed slowed, I followed Ray Allen and Carol and Aunt Gladys to the second pew up front. Doris' boys and other family members who would be playing and singing were up front. I sat at the very end of the pew. Aunt Gladys, still in the wheelchair, was parked in the aisle beside me.

Aunt Gladys knew what was going on. She was weeping. I put my arm around her. Ray Allen was stiff and uncomfortable in his dark suit. He told me that what Aunt Gladys had blurted out was true.

There would be no preacher; that's the way Mama wanted it. She had left instructions in a letter. Eddie, Doris' oldest son, would take charge of the service. I was quite taken aback. But I still didn't know what to expect. I just didn't want a religious frenzy, a call to salvation.

People were still coming in. There were members of the extended family I hadn't even known about. Eddie came over to speak to me just before the service started and explained how it would go. He would sing a duet with his wife Betsey. The two daughters would also sing, and there would be a solo from the youngest boy's wife Beth. But mostly the entire congregation would sing together. "Grandma included the one you like so much, Aunt Betty, 'Fly, Fly, Away,'" Eddie told me.

My heart hurt. For a brief moment I thought I couldn't contain the pain and would break down in spite of myself. But the moment passed. And then the young people gathered up on the altar with their instruments to the right of Mama's casket started playing "Jesus, Hold My Hand" and we all sang through our tears. Eddie and Betsey sang a last duet and then we all joined in with "Fly, Fly, Away." After that Eddie said he wanted to say a few words, and I waited. Was the preaching about to start in earnest? But no, Eddie was simply talking about Mama, what she had meant to him through the years, her care of him and his brothers when his mother went out to work. Little things, like how Mama had fixed each of them his choice of breakfast every morning like a short-order cook, how she fussed over their clothes, how she made them mind, how he always felt safe when she was around. And then Betsey took her turn and talked about Mama, too, what a wonderful grandmother-in-law she had been, how she felt at home with her and how she felt loved by Mama. Then the other boys and their families rose to speak, and Ray

Allen's son recalled how astonished he was, as a little boy, to realize that Mama had other grandchildren he hardly knew about, because she made him and his brother feel they were the only grandchildren she had.

And after that, moved by Mama's presence and the simplicity of the gathering, I went to the front and talked about how I had chosen political expression to guide my life instead of religious expression, and how Mama and I, years ago, had hit upon the solution of holding each other's belief systems hostage: If I didn't speak to her of politics she wouldn't preach to me about religion. It worked because our emotional love for each other overcame our differences, and even in periods of my most extreme rebellion, she never let me go. And all the time I was talking I was weeping, but my voice was steady, and then I couldn't talk anymore and took my seat.

My nephews turned to their instruments once again with a rousing rendition of "His Eye Is On the Sparrow." Halfway through the song the two youngest nephews broke off and came down and wheeled Aunt Gladys up onto the music platform. She used to play the drums with them occasionally. She was helped up on the drummer's seat and given the drumsticks. Would she remember how to play?

Yes. Oh, yes. I started smiling through my tears. Here was Aunt Gladys, her mind largely gone, in a wheelchair but rising to the occasion, playing the drums for Mama. She stayed up there and played along with the band for the rest of the singing. Too soon it was time for the service to close. Aunt Gladys was wheeled back to my side. Beth went to the front and started singing "Amazing Grace" without accompaniment.

As the clear, sweet tones of the young woman's voice filled the chapel, Aunt Gladys began weeping softly. I put my arm around her trembling shoulders. And for the first time in our entire association I felt a surge of warmth toward her, a real affection, along with the sudden realization that one of the reasons I had resented her so much was because I had pushed onto her all of the weaknesses I had struggled against within myself. I could not tolerate sexism, racism, masochism within myself; no, it wasn't me who held these firmly conditioned attitudes, it was her, the evil one, Aunt Gladys.

And then I couldn't recognize her gutsiness, her strength of purpose in taking financial care of herself, her determination to make a buck even in the hardest of times with sheer hard work. She spread the buck around; however grudgingly at times, she did it, she saw that her relatives were never cold or hungry. Several Christmases she was Santa Claus when I was a kid. She bought me my first pair of store-bought panties and paid for my first permanent wave and yes, she taught me to tap-dance ...

But Mama saw Aunt Gladys' strength. In spite of what I considered Mama's stunted intellectual growth because of religion, she had great emotional intelligence. Mama saw to the heart of things. How could she do that? How was that possible? How could a woman who accepted her position in society without fuss or rebellion impact and influence so many people, evoke such love from so many? What is it, Mama, what is it that you had, that still lingers here? Love, oh yes, I know you had love, but it was something else. What was it, that one thing that gave you such emotional strength, that carried you through sleet, storm, hail, floods, poverty, Daddy's illness and death, Doris' sudden departure, my rebellions ... Religion?

No. It wasn't the religion in itself, was it, Mama? I know lots of people who have religion but not much else. It was your determination to live what you believed, to look for the best, to never despair, to stay close to your own inner voice.

Integrity. That's what it was. Integrity. Emotional integrity.

That's what you had that made you a rare bird. And you gave me a thirst for this, this integrity, this need to be one in emotion and action. And while I have needs also for intellectual development, it can't be at the expense of this emotional integrity; that must come along, too. It must, as it is the basis of the other, it is at the heart of the other ...

The song finished. Aunt Gladys turned her face up to me, tear-stained, full of anguish.

I kissed her on the forehead. "I love you," I whispered.

"What?"

"I said 'I love you.'"

She nodded. "I know. Can we get something to eat now?"

That's it, I think, as the memory of Mama's funeral fades before my eyes. I am back in my prison cell trying to think of the best way to present my thoughts about sentencing to Mr. Justice Parrett. That's what I had forgotten, why I have been going over and over that last summer with Mama and Aunt Gladys, trying to recapture something, some kernel of truth that I need now, right now, in this situation I am in. It is Mama's emotional integrity. Her gift of the preacherless funeral edged me up a notch in understanding. My struggle must always centre on walking my talk, and to do that I must work constantly to combine emotional integrity with intellectual integrity. Now I know what I will say to the judge in the morning.

◆

I take my turn at the courtroom podium:

"Sir, I deeply regret that I appear before you in this court on the charge of criminal contempt of court. In my final arguments before you last week I addressed my dismay concerning how citizens like me, who protest the destruction of the Elaho by Interfor logging company, are discriminated against by the policies of the Attorney General's office, who instructs the RCMP not to arrest us under the Criminal Code, which would allow us to bring in why we are driven by conscience to put our bodies on the line in the effort to save something of our ancient forests.

"By arresting us under court-ordered injunction we are then left defenceless, as the only issue before the court becomes one of did we or did we not break the injunction. In this way, protesters like me are left defenceless and the original reason for the arrests in the first place, which is the destruction of old-growth forests, in this case the Elaho, is left almost unmentioned in the courtroom and is certainly without legal counsel, so to speak. It's almost as though the Elaho doesn't really exist. It's as though the only real, tangible, important entity here is the court-ordered injunction. This injunction assumes a profound profile and supersedes the rights of the accused; it supersedes the very notion of democracy and it supersedes the ancient forests of the Elaho Valley itself. We are all brought low before the might of the court-ordered injunction.

"But I hope for a better day. I long for the day when any citizen, like myself, who is fed up with the way corporate values are destroying this earth, can stand in front of a logging truck or climb a tree and refuse to come down or prepare food in a peace camp or do a hundred other protest things and be charged only for their actions and not for contempt of court. I long for the day when SLAPP suits and the court injunctions that arise out of them will be abolished. About sentencing, specifically my own sentencing, sir, I leave that in your hands. I am responsible for my own actions ..."

Should I put in here something about the devil didn't make me blockade Interfor logging trucks? Yes, as I have written it on the copy I have given to the judge. I talk about how this decision was my own and nobody else's, and then I talk about being a political prisoner.

"Sir, when I am in jail I consider myself a political prisoner, and I act accordingly. I write letters and send them around the world and advise anyone even remotely interested that I am a political prisoner in Canada, a country that isn't supposed to have political prisoners. And I tell them why I am in prison in Canada.

"Sir, Canada has one of the highest incarceration rates in the Western world, which is a disgrace. And I consider most of the women in prison in Burnaby also to be political prisoners. The decision to imprison sick, drug-addicted women instead of providing the resources they need to get well is a political decision, a disgusting decision; it is to say that there are people in this society who deserve nothing because they are nothing, that it is okay to throw away certain people, just as it is okay to throw away irreplaceable old-growth forests like the Elaho.

"Well, it is not okay with me, sir. The Native people of old called the trees in the forests of old the Standing Ones. And we, sir, as well as the Natives, all of us, evolved together down through the ages with these forests, these trees; our very breathing is synchronized, we breathe in what they breathe out; they need our breath to grow and mature, become ancient, thousands of years ancient, fall down, become nursery logs and start the life cycle over again. When we make deserts of these forests we make deserts of our own hearts and spirits and degrade the entire human race.

"Sir, I was raised in a rainforest. When I was a child the entire area of southern Louisiana was one series of swamps, wetlands, bayous, wildlife so thick and plentiful sometimes you couldn't see the sky for the migrating of birds. I grew up with alligators, pelicans and wild cats, with creeks and streams so full of catfish and crayfish no one need ever go hungry. This was before the logging, before the cutting of the cypress groves, before the felling of the mighty oaks, before the draining and filling in and melting away of the wetlands. Today for the first time in the history of southern Louisiana there is a drought upon the land, a drought going into its third year. Two-thirds of the wetlands are gone, as is most of the wildlife, and the summers have become so hot that even born and bred Southerners are wondering if they have already died and gone to hell."

I pause. At this point I thank all of the lawyers, including Mr. Flanz, Crown Counsel, all the courtroom employees who have shown me so many small kindnesses, and then I thank my co-accused and say that the ones who went out to the Elaho to try to protect her have my unfailing loyalty and respect. Then I turn to face Barney and the others and tell them that while they may not be heroes to this court, they are heroes to me and will always be. And then I continue my address to Mr. Justice Parrett.

"In reality, sir, the only real freedom that anyone actually finds is within the confines of one's own mind and spirit. It sounds trite, I know, but that kind of freedom really can't be imprisoned. You can put me in jail, sir, but I will not be your prisoner. I will not be

Interfor's prisoner, or a prisoner of the Attorney General or a prisoner of these nice sheriffs, or a prisoner of Burnaby Correctional Centre for Women. I am a prisoner of my own conscience, sir, and only of my own conscience, and that makes me a free woman, a free person. And as a free person I refuse to enter into any sort of collusion with this court in terms of potential conditions or undertakings or electronic monitoring as part of sentencing. Not that I think any will be offered, but just in case."

Here I go on to list the specific conditions I will not accept, including community service work. I tell Mr. Justice Parrett that I have done more than my share of community service work in my life—I have done it freely, for love, and I refuse to have it imposed upon me as punishment.

"I will never be a party," I continue, "to assisting in my own punishment in ways that would force me to internalize prison, to internalize confinement, to internalize guilt, to internalize the power of Interfor and the Attorney General's office to punish me for trying to protect public property, property that every citizen has a right, and not just a right, but also a duty, to protect and enjoy and respect and love. Sir, you must lock me up, or let me go."

There. With the delivery of those words I walk back to the prisoner's box. Amidst a standing ovation. The other prisoners and I have wonderful support from our friends. There are four of us sitting on the prisoners' bench now, including Barney Kern. Rick McCallion gives his address to the judge, followed by Barney. Then we are all finished.

It is now up to Mr. Justice Parrett. We have a court break and I am taken up to the courthouse cells and locked down. I feel calm enough. I'm probably looking at six months, I think. I'll miss the little ones—

my grandchildren. They all live on Vancouver Island. I'll be sent back to the women's prison in Burnaby. But six months isn't the end of the world, even with no remission, I tell myself. After all, I did four and a half months during the Clayoquot blockades. But there is a waiting inside me.

Court finally reconvenes. The room is full of friends, relatives and supporters. The love and concern radiating from them is almost tangible. The media is also there. Mr. Justice Parrett enters. We all rise. He sits behind his big desk. The rest of us sit, too. The tension is rising. Mr. Justice Parrett begins to read from his prepared text. Rick McCallion and Dennis Porter will be sentenced on October 30, 2000, for civil contempt. The remaining five of us will be sentenced forthwith.

And then he gets down to the nitty-gritty.

"Justin Paine, Reasha Wolfe and Christopher Keats, will you please stand. Mr. Paine, you have served 18 days in jail since being arrested for breaching the terms of your undertaking to this court. Giving you credit for that time served, I sentence you to serve two months in jail.

"Reasha Wolfe, I sentence you to a term of imprisonment of three months.

"Christopher Keats, having taken into account all of your personal circumstances, I order suspended the passing of sentence upon you and direct that you be released on a probation order for a period of one year containing the standard provisions that you keep the peace and be of good behaviour. That disposition will allow you to return to Ontario. Please be seated.

"Mr. Kern and Ms. Krawczyk, would you please stand." From the prisoner's box, Barney and I stand.

"For your roles in these events and, in particular, the extent to which your actions and attitudes have been reflected in your public statements, you have left me little option. I sentence each of you to a term of imprisonment of one year. These are contempt sentences. I specifically direct that each of these accused serve the time to which they have been sentenced."

Wow. A whole year! Without remission time. Mr. Justice Parrett has just given my definition of a mean ole man new depth and dimension. He has just condemned me to an entire year of Rock 101! An entire year of pushing buzzers to be allowed through doorways, an entire year of periodic lockdowns, a year of no hot peppers, no tap shoes, no dental floss, no word processor, nobody at my beck and call who loves me.

The courtroom is buzzing with angry comments hurled at the judge. Suddenly the room is ringed with sheriffs. Yet I remain calm. I feel composed, even peaceful, for I go armed now with an elder's fully awakened sense of responsibility reinforced with my own intellectual pursuits and strengthened by a heightened awareness that my mother has somehow wrapped me in her own emotional grounding. I feel it's a winning combination. In fact, prison walls cannot contain such a combination, nor can legal or judicial authorities control it. Bring on the year of incarceration without remission! I am girded for battle! I am invincible!

I am also being hustled out of the courtroom by the sheriffs. But I turn at the heavy door that leads up to the cells.

"It isn't over yet!" I yell at the packed courtroom. "It isn't over yet!"

"We love you!" friends and supporters shout back in unison as I am taken away with the others.

And that will have to be enough. For the moment.

Afterword

I appealed the year's prison sentence handed down to me by Mr. Justice Parrett. After serving four months in the Burnaby Correctional Centre for Women, I won my appeal and was released without conditions.

Glenn Orris, the appeal lawyer who was retained on my behalf by supporters in the environmental community, did a fine job in my defence. I would have been just as happy to represent myself in the appeal process, as I had done in the trial, but my friends in Greenpeace, the Friends of Clayoquot Sound and Forest Ethics all voiced concern that the year's sentence Barney Kern and I had received must not be allowed to set a precedent. They persuaded me to allow Mr. Orris to represent me.

My own approach to civil disobedience was and remains different than the position taken by defence and appeal lawyers and most of my environmentalist friends. I welcomed a harsh sentence because the very harshness immediately threw into bold relief the inherent injustice in how British Columbia's judicial system deals with citizens who dare to directly challenge logging corporations. And the harshness of my sentence brought worldwide attention to the rapaciousness of logging companies like Interfor, which plunder the public forests and then insist that taxpayers clean up the mess they leave behind. Clearcutting is a crime against nature and all her species, and I keep this thought before me whenever I am faced with the armed might of the logging companies, the courts and the prisons of British Columbia.

Of all of the men who took part in the attack on the protest camp in the Elaho Valley, only five were eventually charged. All five were convicted. However, not even one of these men who trashed and burned the camp, who beat up three of the peaceful demonstrators so badly that they had to be taken to hospital, served any jail time, not even a day. They were all given suspended sentences. Madam Justice Ellen Burdett, the presiding judge, said in sentencing that there was "at least tacit corporate approval" of the attack, but she didn't see fit to give either the officers of Interfor or the workers a look at the inside of a jail cell. So much for my notion that women judges might bring a little much-needed justice into the courtroom. Still, my young environmentalist friends and I are undeterred. Suzanne Jackson, Barney Kern, Rick McCallion and most of the Elaho defenders are still involved with our public forests in one way or another.

As this book goes to press, the situation in the Elaho Valley is relatively quiet. Some logging is continuing south of the Lava Creek bridge but not in the north of the valley, where the ancient Douglas firs stand. This is thanks in large part to the Squamish Nation and to Chief Bill Williams, who is both elected and hereditary chief. The Squamish First Nations people have brought forth a land-use plan that prohibits clearcutting the forests north of the Lava Creek bridge. Interfor has not signed onto this plan as yet, but neither has it rejected it. Meanwhile our newly elected provincial Liberal government has promised to increase the annual allowable cutting of trees by at least twenty percent, so the battle in the woods in British Columbia is not over.

My family is supportive of my activism in the forests, but they worry nevertheless. They worry most when I am out in the woods blockading. Marian, my youngest daughter, has accompanied me on several of these occasions and realizes that there is the ever-present danger of being on the receiving end of an irate logger's wrath. When I am actually arrested and taken off to jail, my family breathes a collective sigh of relief. They assume that in prison nothing much can happen to me that I can't handle, except possibly that I may be driven mad by a rock 'n' roll radio station.

As I write this my family is well, including my son Andy, who has returned to his life's passion of music with a renewed appreciation of life itself. My Aunt Gladys survived my mother by only a couple of months. She passed away peacefully in the nursing home with her nephews by her side.

I spent the long months in prison after sentencing primarily reading, writing and thinking. Thinking about the role of elders, the role of women, the role of mothers. That is the focus of my current writing, because at age seventy-three I sometimes get the feeling I'm mother to just about everybody.

When I was released from prison I was interviewed by provincial and national radio and television, and the question continually arose, Did I consider myself a martyr or a hero? My answer was neither. I am not a martyr or a hero, but for a brief time I did become a kind of conduit for the average British Columbian's concerns about the clearcutting of our public forests. For this period of time I was able to articulate the grief and outrage most people feel when they behold a ruined and bleeding mountain, a trashed salmon stream or a dying grizzly bear population. I am glad I was able to serve this function, and I intend to persevere. This struggle has only begun.

Acknowledgements

I wish to thank some of the people, environmental groups and organizations who nourished me emotionally and mentally while I was incarcerated. My first acknowledgement is to Barney Kern and the loosely organized ad hoc committee that became known as the Friends of the Elaho. Greenpeace Canada and Greenpeace International also came to play a significant role in my protest and were largely responsible for the veritable mountain of mail I received from home and abroad. At Greenpeace Canada I especially want to thank Gavin Edwards and Catherine Stewart for their efforts in keeping me connected to the outside world while I was in prison.

Although the Western Canada Wilderness Committee does not engage in civil disobedience, I want to thank Joe Foy and Paul George for their comprehensive knowledge of the ecosystems of the Elaho Valley and for their readiness to teach me about these ecosystems and the history of the area. I am most grateful for the friendship and support of Shelley Vine, who first visited me in prison in 1993 while filming *The Fury of the Sound: Women of the Clayoquot* and who remained steadfast throughout my Elaho trials and imprisonment. I also want to thank Tzeporah Berman of Forest Ethics for her valuable assistance. Valerie Langer and the entire office of Friends of Clayoquot Sound gave seasoned advice and comfort and accepted all my long distance collect telephone calls. I also appreciate the discus-

sions surrounding my incarceration and the letters written on my behalf by many groups of elders, including several groups of Raging
Grannies and some members of the Council of Elders of the David
Suzuki Foundation. My special thanks to the Raging Grannies, who
went to Germany on behalf of the public forests of British Columbia,
and on my behalf.

I want to express my gratitude to Robert Moore-Stewart, my
friend and legal counsel, who has worked with me through various
court appearances, often without pay, and who profoundly under-
stands the nature of protest.

I want to express appreciation to my children for their support of
my protest actions, particularly to my youngest daughter Marian,
who sang with me on the road blockade in the Elaho and who shoul-
dered the burden of keeping our mutual home fires burning while I
was in Burnaby Correctional Centre for Women. Marian isn't especially keen about my writing about her, but then none of my children
are keen about my writing about them. I want to take this opportunity to advise Joe, Mike, Andy, Susan, Margaret Elizabeth, Rose
Mary, Barbara Ellen and Marian that I write about them because I
find them so interesting. Besides, they all have great humour
genes, and where else, as a writer, could I find such witty, convenient
subjects?

I want to thank the letter writers of the world whose letters and
cards drove the correctional staff at BCCW to ask me to log the incoming mail myself as they couldn't keep up with the volume. The
letters eventually numbered over a thousand, coming from England,
Germany, Scotland, Ireland, Greece, Italy, France, the Netherlands,
Switzerland, Puerto Rico, Guatemala and the outback of Australia, as
well as from every Canadian province and territory and from many

American states. To all of these people I want to say: Your outpour-
ing of emotional support was one of the most wonderful and welcome surprises of my entire life.

I want to give a special thanks to my friend and agent, Monica
Marcovici, who lives and breathes environmental issues and who
rarely missed a visiting day while I was incarcerated in Burnaby
Correctional Centre for Women. Her steadfast friendship and cheery
optimism helped me through that incredibly contentious time, and
her belief in my protests and in my manuscript was, and remains,
unfailing.

I want to thank my editor, Barbara Kuhne, who patiently explained, much to my chagrin, that the book would only improve by
deleting some of my more litigious rants. I complained at the time,
but she is used to that, so I eventually graciously gave way to her
more objective, seasoned judgement.

And last but not least, thank you Raincoast Books. You're the
greatest.

I feel blessed to have touched so many people, and to be touched
by them in return. For I have come to believe that it is only in this
reaching out and touching each other that we can actually come to
know each other and to find the strength to build a new world.

About the Author

Betty Krawczyk was born in California in the middle of the Depression and she was raised in Baton Rouge, Louisiana. She started writing in 1960, emigrated to Canada in 1966, and has written for numerous publications including the *Vancouver Sun* and various Greenpeace magazines. Betty has been pulled into many social struggles, including protests against segregation and the Vietnam war, and to protect civil and women's rights. Finally, just as she was about to "retire" in peaceful Clayoquot Sound, British Columbia, she found herself fighting for the democratic right to protect the wilderness. On September 15, 2000 Betty was sentenced to one year in jail without parole for blockading a road in the Elaho, British Columbia. She was released in 2001.

More Fine Non-Fiction Titles *from* Raincoast Books

Paddling Through Time • *Joanna Streetly* • *Photographs by Adrian Dorst*

In vivid words and breathtaking colour photos, Streetly and Dorst depict the allure of Clayoquot Sound, one of the world's finest natural reserves. The book is the result of a week-long trip by kayak through the area and combines present-day impressions with stories of the region's colourful past, from Native culture and traditions to high-profile confrontations between forest companies and environmentalists. Here is an inspirational and beautiful portrait of a unique area of the world, recognized by the United Nations as a World Heritage Ecosystem.

1-55192-278-9 • $29.95 CDN/$21.95 USA

Hiking on the Edge: Revised Third Edition • *Ian Gill*
Photographs by David Nunuk

A journey in pictures and words along the West Coast Trail. With a revised section on the Juan de Fuca Marine Trail and updated information, this book is the definitive resource for both the armchair traveller and the veteran hiker interested in venturing to the western edge of British Columbia's Vancouver Island.

1-55192-502-2 • $29.95 CDN/$18.95 USA

Cabin at Singing River • *Chris Czajkowski* • *Foreword by Peter Gzowski*

This new, redesigned edition of a classic account of frontier life shows how one woman accomplished the task of building her own home and making a slight, human indentation in a remote and uninhabited spot in the interior of British Columbia. "Czajkowski has followed a different path, reminding us of how much we don't need, and how much we are missing." —*The Globe and Mail*

1-55192-463-3 • $21.95 CDN/$15.95 USA

A Pour of Rain: Stories from a West Coast Fort • *Helen Meilleur*

This classic is one of the best accounts we have of the first non-Native settlers on Canada's Northwest coast. Fort Simpson—where author Helen Meilleur was born in 1910—was built in 1831 about 1,500 kilometres north of Vancouver. *A Pour of Rain* combines personal memoir of an early twentieth-century childhood with a well-researched, carefully reconstructed history of the fort in the mid-nineteenth century when it dealt with tribal wars, wrecked ships and the arrival of missionaries and gold-seekers.

155192-422-6 • $24.95 CDN/$18.95 USA